Who Are These People?

Book Two

Deb Gorman

Who Are These People?

Spiritual Lessons Learned In Obscurity

Book Two

DEB GORMAN

Who Are These People?
Book Two

Edited by Dori Harrell - Breakout Editing
(http://doriharrell.wix.com/breakoutediting)
Cover design by Emilie Hendryx
(http://www.eacreativedesign.jimdo.com)
Author's photograph by Ric Brunstetter, RBIII Studios
Formatting by Rik Hall, Wild Seas Formatting
(http://www.WildSeasFormatting.com)

ISBN 978-0-9979587-3-7 (Paperback)
ISBN 978-0-9979587-2-0 (Digital)

Published by Deb Gorman
Debo Publishing
www.debggorman.com

Contents

Acknowledgments i

Introduction iv

Chapter 1 The God Who Sees Me 1

Chapter 2 The Scarlet Rope 29

Chapter 3 By Night 75

Chapter 4 Living Water 117

Chapter 5 The Tree 141

Chapter 6 Pardoned 181

Acknowledgments

It's always hard to acknowledge *everyone* who has had a hand in getting a story out to readers. There are so many people who have encouraged me, listened to me agonize over minutiae, and read bits and pieces of these stories and yearned to hear the rest.

I work and worship with some very good friends who have been waiting for me to finish this manuscript—and they've let me know the first book in this series was not enough. They want more. You know who you are!

I thank my pastor, Jim Merillat, for some very timely and encouraging words he spoke to me not long ago. He spoke the words God knew I needed to hear in that moment.

Thank you to my family. It's not easy to have a mother, grandmother, wife, sister, and daughter who holes up in her writing cave for hours on end. You folks ground me and remind me that this life is about relationships—and you're not talking about the one I have with my laptop!

I also thank the professionals with whom I worked to get these stories into book form, and I thank you, my readers.

To all my author friends on Facebook, thank you for your encouragement and help. Writers are truly wonderful human beings who understand the needs of an introvert. There's a wonderful quote I saw posted by one author friend. "Writing: a profession for introverts who want to tell you a story but don't want to make eye contact while telling it" (source unknown). That says it all. Authors understand authors, and I'm privileged to learn from all of you.

My editor, Dori Harrell, Breakout Editing, has become a colleague as well as a dear friend. She knows my voice, my heart, and my passion. She's a consummate professional, and I can safely trust her to edit wisely while helping me to say what God has given me to say.

My cover designer, Emilie Hendryx, is a talented photographer and artist and instinctively knows what I'm looking for. Thank you.

My formatter, Rik Hall, Wild Seas Formatting, is fast, accurate, and a joy to work with.

To our German shepherd, Hoka, who listens patiently from her perch on the love seat in my office as I talk to people only I can see and hear—I love your beautiful ears and your lovely soul.

And I save the best for last. To my Redeemer, Friend, and Savior, the One who calls me and equips me, and who will someday take my hand and lead me to His side, Jesus the Christ—thank You for living and dying for me. Thank you for giving my life purpose, for seeing my tears, for helping me journey through the shadowlands. I can't wait to get home.

To my father, Bruce R. Drake, who taught me to choose wisely and live with integrity.

Introduction

Today I have given you the choice between life and death, between blessings and curses. Now I call on heaven and earth to witness the choice you make. Oh, that you would choose life, so that you and your descendants might live!
And now, Israel, what does the Lord your God require of you? He requires only that you fear the Lord your God, and live in a way that pleases him, and love him and serve him with all your heart and soul. And you must always obey the Lord's commands and decrees that I am giving you today for your own good.
(Deuteronomy 30:19; 10:12, 13)

***

Choices, choices! Our lives, from birth to death, are composed largely of choices. Some are made for us, and some we make ourselves. Some are life changing. Some only change the moment in which we now exist.

Where shall we eat?

Where shall we shop for our new car? What kind should we buy?

Where shall I go to school?

In which neighborhood shall we look for a house?

Shall I get a plain coffee or a latte?

Is this the person I should marry?

The choices we make shape our lives. If we could look at the past with the eyes of an artist, we would see that each choice is a brushstroke, filling in the canvas of our lives with brilliant colors and promises or the gray of uncertainty and unfulfilled expectations. The people we read about in God's Word were no different than us.

The biblical characters included in these stories had choices to make. Abram and Sarai made a choice to go to Egypt during a famine—and met Hagar. Rahab, an Amorite woman, decided to help two Hebrew spies—and was thereafter placed in the human lineage of Messiah. The Samaritan woman chose to lay down *her* water jar and draw from a different spring—and impacted her entire village.

God placed these ordinary people and their stories into His Word for a reason. Some span several verses or chapters, some only a few verses. We are left wondering who they really were, what they might have looked like, what we can learn from them.

God never wastes anything—not even space on a page. He wants us to know Him, and He is the supreme storyteller!

This is a work of creative nonfiction, based upon real people and the truth of God's Word. In these pages, I have attempted to fill in the canvas of their lives in order to help us understand the lessons God has for us.

As you read, I encourage you to ask God what He wants you to learn about the choices you have made and will have to make in the future. It's been said that wisdom is knowing what's really important in life and understanding that some things really don't matter. This I believe, and I would add that there's only one thing in this life that matters: a vibrant, growing relationship with Jesus Christ.

And I leave you with this, from an unnamed source: the path of your life will change each time you determine to hold fast to your faith.

Deb Gorman

Chapter 1
The God Who Sees Me

The eternal God is your refuge, and his everlasting arms are under you.
—Deuteronomy 33:27

Babak, the pharaoh's chief vizier, tried to make himself smaller as the god on earth, Huni, strode angrily into the room where his viziers awaited, in his haste not even bothering to make sure the door closed properly. Voice thundering in spite of his relatively small stature, Huni made an impressive display of power—power he'd grasped for himself some years back when he'd arrived in Memphis and taken it for his own city, naming himself pharaoh.

"Why must I be plagued with these filthy desert dwellers?" Huni shouted, sweat dripping on his brow.

Babak's gaze slipped around the council room at the men whose very lives, like his own, depended upon the unpredictable moods of this pharaoh. They all knew better than to give an answer to his question. In spite of their positions as advisers, Huni wasn't asking for their advice. A pharaoh, even a minor one, never asked advice except from the gods. And even that was only a perfunctory courtesy—they usually did what they wanted anyway. Babak guessed Huni had not even consulted Ptah, the principal god of Memphis, over this latest affront to his royal dignity.

"They keep coming and coming. They want and they want. Is there no other pharaoh in Egypt but me? No, don't answer that! I know the answer well enough."

Huni paced back and forth furiously, shoving furniture out

of his way, rudely shouldering his trembling viziers aside, not caring that one fell to his knees.

"I don't care if the gods have sent a famine to their land! These vagabond travelers deplete my storehouses. I'll not suffer this tribe who waits in my courtyard. Send them away!" Huni pointed at the two who guarded the door to his council room.

"You! Tell them to go somewhere else. They'll get nothing from me!"

Then he turned and strode to the window overlooking his city. He surveyed the horizon with his back to them, hands on his hips, as if the matter was settled and nothing further needed to be said.

Babak and the other viziers stood in awkward silence for a moment.

After staying the guards with his hand, Babak timidly approached Huni and, sinking to his knees, spoke up. "Most Worshipful One, may I speak?"

A barely discernible nod from Huni.

"Perhaps, and only perhaps, my lord," Babak began, eyes pointed to the floor, "you should reconsider. Have you seen the woman who travels with this desert chieftain?"

"Woman, what woman?" Huni grunted disagreeably.

"The light-skinned one, Majesty."

"Yes. What about her?"

"She's very beautiful, don't you think?" Nodding heads around him emboldened Babak to say more.

"She would make a most desirable addition to your royal *harim*, would she not?"

Fists clenched and not even turning to face his groveling servant, Huni roared, "By all the gods in the heavens, I should skin you myself, Babak! Isn't she his wife? I may not want to give him aid, but neither do I want to incur the wrath of my gods or his!"

Babak blanched at Huni's tone. But he had information Huni needed, and knowing his pharaoh's appetites well, he gathered his courage and replied quietly, "No, she's not, Majesty. The chieftain says she's his sister."

Huni turned at that, a tight smile playing around his lips. He reached down and hauled Babak to his feet, keeping a strong grip on the other man's collar.

His face inches from Babak's, he growled in a menacing tone that froze Babak's soul. "Is this true, Babak? Or are you just trying to appease my anger? I swear—if I find you are lying, I'll kill you slowly in the most excruciating way!" He tightened his grip on Babak's tunic, twisting it against Babak's neck.

The viziers took a step back, as if trying to distance themselves from the wretched Babak and their all-powerful pharaoh-god.

"I swear it's true. The chieftain said so himself—to me!" Babak rasped out, choking under Huni's grip.

Huni stared into Babak's face a moment longer. Then in a lightning-quick change of mood, he let go of Babak's collar, backed away, and laughed out loud. Babak slumped against the pharaoh's massive desk, clutching his neck.

"Well, this changes everything!" Huni said delightedly, rubbing his large hands together.

An almost audible release of tension whispered in the room as his viziers relaxed.

"Bring this so-called chieftain to me! Immediately!"

The room emptied as Huni's advisers scattered to do his bidding.

Babak walked slowly away from the council chamber, rubbing his neck and trying to clear his throat. *That was a most narrow escape!*

Earlier, Babak had seen two small girls hiding in an alcove around the corner from pharaoh's council chamber. He'd ignored them. As Babak and his cohorts scurried away, Babak looked back and saw the two giggling girls dart in the opposite direction, no doubt taking with them the juiciest gossip in months to share in the women's quarters of the palace.

No matter, Babak thought. *I have but one mission now. Acquire the chieftain's sister for my pharaoh, which will significantly enhance my position.*

Politics are the same everywhere, in any era. Men and women jostle for complete power and control over the masses. The only difference between then and now is the packaging: today, politicians wear tailored suits and plaster their professionally made-up faces all over social media. In Huni's day they wore robes and glittering headdresses and had busts made of themselves placed in strategic public places to remind the masses who controlled them.

There is much scholarly disagreement over exactly when Abram and Sarai went to Egypt during this famine, where they went, and the name of the pharaoh from whom Abram begged help. Some scholars place this event between 2001 BC and 1901 BC. Others place it much earlier than that.

In addition, there were multitudes of Egyptian leaders naming themselves *pharaoh* throughout the earliest known ages. For this story, I went with Huni, who supposedly ruled from Memphis in the Nile Delta region, as the likeliest pharaoh for this biblical event in Abram's life.

Huni's name means *smiter*, and he was probably the last ruler of Egypt's Third Dynasty. He was a builder of pyramids and fortresses, working to consolidate his power in the region, snubbing his nose at traditional places to build. He was a mover and a shaker in his day.

Pharaohs in those times had multiple wives and concubines in order to ensure their family lines would continue to govern. Many children meant stability of rule. Huni was no exception.

And it was to this pharaoh that Abram brought his family in time of need. It could be said that Abram went to Egypt without counsel from God, that he gave in to fear and should have asked God where to go for provision. Many biblical scholars say this very thing. One wonders what course history would have taken had he not gone to Egypt, lied about his relationship with Sarai, and acquired Hagar as a slave. Maybe current events would be without Middle East hostilities if Abram had just knelt in prayer before heading south.

All those speculations, however, are moot. Hagar is a reality of our history, and the thing we must do with it is to understand what her story means to us. Her *spiritual lessons learned in obscurity* were placed in the Scriptures for our instruction and training in righteousness.

Let's dive in...

The next day saw changes in the women's quarters of Huni's palace. A new arrival caused a stir among the wives and daughters of Huni and the other serving women who lived there. The gossip carried by the two giggling eavesdroppers had indeed been truth.

Sarai was installed in her own quarters, given a handmaiden, and then left alone. She was watched with curiosity by Hagar and her sisters, and with suspicion by Huni's wives. They envied her beauty. She had the light skin so prized by the pharaohs, delicate features, and a dainty stature. Her long, luxurious hair was dressed modestly, without the glitter usually adorned by Egyptian women of high standing.

Hagar in particular watched her with interest. She was strange, exotic; her mysterious dark eyes held secrets. She gazed with interest at her new surroundings. Though a desert tent dweller, she carried herself like a princess, showing no fear.

No wonder Father is taken with her.

Sarai caught Hagar's sly glances and beckoned her. At first Hagar was too timid to approach this strange woman, but Sarai had kindness upon her face, so Hagar stepped to within a few feet of her and then glanced quickly around to see if anyone was watching. Only her sisters stared her way. Hagar took one step forward, now standing directly in front of Sarai, who sat on her sleeping mat as regally as any queen on her throne.

"What is your name, child?" Sarai asked in her strange accent. Hagar understood enough of the question though.

"My name is Hagar, and I'm the daughter of the pharaoh, bless him," Hagar said proudly, stretching herself up to her full height.

Sarai gazed at Hagar, an unreadable expression on her face. *Is it sympathy? Why?*

" And do you seek refuge, little Hagar, as the meaning of your name suggests?" Sarai asked.

Hagar was astonished. *How does she – a foreigner – know the meaning of my name?*

"I have no need of refuge, tent dweller!" she replied haughtily. "I'm the daughter of Huni, pharaoh of Memphis! What need have I of refuge?"

Sarai smiled sweetly at Hagar and said, "We all have need of refuge, my little Hagar. The God of Israel is mine. Who is yours?" Sarai's voice was low and gentle, but her dark eyes, glittering in the torchlight, burned with passion.

"Hagar! Do not speak to the slave!"

The command came out of nowhere. A moment ago, her only audience was her sisters, but as Hagar turned swiftly, she now saw Sabah, the mistress of the women's quarters and her father's principal wife, glaring at her.

"Slave, Sabah? I thought she was to be Father's wife," Hagar challenged, not wishing to be chastised like a child before this foreign woman.

"She's not his wife yet, little one. Now obey me and come away." Sabah's tone suggested immediate repercussions would be in order should Hagar disobey.

Hagar turned back to Sarai and said in a whisper, "My pharaoh and the god Ptah are my refuge. They're all I need!"

As she spun and walked swiftly away in obedience to Sabah, the gently whispered voice of Sarai floated to her ears.

"We'll speak again, little Hagar. I'm sure of it."

Hagar oft remembered the whispered words during the next weeks and wondered what they meant. She didn't speak to Sarai again but watched her surreptitiously whenever she got the chance. Sarai was always kind, always gracious, never haughty, but she didn't comport herself as a victim either. She was a strange mix of slave and princess. Even as she endured the ritual preparations to become wife of the pharaoh, preparations likely to continue for a year before she was taken to his bed, Sarai carried herself with a quiet dignity. Hagar found her oddly attractive, a woman she would like to know. As the weeks went on, she found herself hoping that her father would indeed marry this woman—*perhaps I'll call her mother*. Of all her father's wives, none were her mother.

It was not to be.

***

"Bring that miserable desert dweller to me! Now!" Huni's voice thundered from his bedchamber. He heard the scurrying feet of his guards as they retreated from his door to do his bidding.

He sat up in his bed and scratched again at the white patches on his forearms and legs. The scourge had spread to his abdomen and back since yesterday and showed no signs of healing. He'd heard that the strange plague, which baffled his physicians and magicians, had spread throughout his household. And now, on the dawn of this new day, he had to admit the reason.

His mind reeled at the dream he'd had. The voice that had spoken to him was entirely unfamiliar. His heart told him it was a deity, but his intellect refused to acknowledge it. Ptah never spoke to him audibly, but Huni knew it was not *his* voice in the dream.

Huni did not want to believe what his magicians told him just a few days ago. How wrong he'd been to discount their admonitions! Through their wisdom and their magic arts, they'd learned what this deity told him last night—that Sarai was the *wife* of the desert rat. Sister, yes, according to the custom of Abram's people to "adopt" their wives to confer legal inheritance upon them, but she was also his *wife*! Beautiful as she was, she could never be Huni's. And now he and his whole household were suffering because of his own arrogance in not listening to his advisers.

When questioned, Sarai had confirmed it. Huni was beyond angry. He was enraged, not only because of his foreign-relations predicament but because of his wounded pride.

Huni got up from his bed and hobbled—the miserable disease now attacked his muscles—to his armoire to get dressed. He heard a voice outside his door. He recognized it as Babak's.

"My lord, may I assist you in dressing?" Babak's wheedling voice inquired.

"No! Stay out!" Huni shouted. He did not want Babak's pity or Huni's weakened condition to be reported.

"Get Tahlahl in here. I need to speak with him. And make sure he's admitted before the foreigner!" Huni's voice brooked no argument.

Babak's footsteps echoed down the hallway.

Moments later a soft knock sounded on the door to Huni's private chamber. Tahlahl slipped inside. Tahlahl was a slight man with an intelligent face. Huni had come to trust his judgment on many matters. Tahlahl approached Huni and dropped to his knees immediately. Huni bade him arise and began pacing angrily.

"I had a dream, Tahlahl. You're the wisest man in my kingdom. I must know what to do." Huni noted the immediate spark of interest on Tahlahl's face. Huni knew Tahlahl's ambition—he no doubt weighed in his mind the opportunity now handed to him.

"What was the dream, Majesty?"

"It was a voice—of man or god I could not tell—informing me that the sickness plaguing my household is because I took the desert-rat's *wife*! My magicians were correct. But how was I to know? I was told point blank by Babak that the woman is his sister. I'm innocent in this!"

He didn't try to hide his desperation. "Give me your best advice, Tahlahl. Look at me!" Huni bared both forearms.

Blanching at the white rottenness spreading on the skin of his pharaoh, Tahlahl turned abruptly and walked to the door and placed his ear against it. He turned, eyes narrowed and a finger to his lips, and strode back to Huni's side, leaning close to him.

"Send Babak on an errand, my lord. He eavesdrops," Tahlahl said quietly.

Head shaking in anger, Huni shouted, "Babak! I'm hungry! Get me some goat's meat! And make sure it's thoroughly cooked this time!" Again, the scurrying footsteps could be heard retreating.

Huni turned and watched Tahlahl, who gazed out the window with one hand cupped on his cheek. Patience was not one of Huni's virtues, but he stilled himself and waited. Several minutes passed.

With a sigh, Tahlahl turned and locked eyes with his pharaoh.

"You must get rid of Babak. Today. You are god on earth in this city, and you were duped. Your power must not be allowed to weaken in the eyes of your people. And then you must send these foreigners away with much plunder. I believe it was their god who spoke to you, and this god has graciously given you a way out of this mess created by Babak, a way that will allow your life and your dignity to remain. And we must hope the plagues will stop once you restore his wife to him and send him on his way." Tahlahl stopped, eyeing Huni warily, noting the suffusion of purple on his face.

"So I'm to reward this desert scum for his lie? You can't be serious! How does this advance my power?"

Tahlahl chose his words carefully. "Majesty, a small concession now does not mean you will be unable to exact retribution in the future. Right now, your dignity and power must be protected. And then, someday, perhaps Ptah will guide you to a well-deserved reckoning with this deceiver."

Huni thought for a moment and then exhaled slowly. "All right, Tahlahl, I will take your advice. And I will leave it to you to dispatch the miserable Babak—a task I'm sure you will accomplish with delight and discretion."

Huni's eyes burned into Tahlahl's. Unflinching, Tahlahl returned the look.

"Who would you propose take Babak's place?" Huni asked.

Not hesitating for a moment, Tahlahl replied, "Kagemni, Majesty. He is manageable, a writer of scrolls, intelligent."

He didn't add *unambitious,* but to Huni's sharp ears, it was clearly implied. *Tahlahl indeed knows his sovereign's mind.* Huni thought briefly of elevating *him* to Babak's position but discarded the notion. Tahlahl was too valuable in his present duty of covert intelligence and dispatcher of ambitious viziers.

Hearing muted noises through the door, Huni signaled Tahlahl to open it. Babak stood there with a plate of steaming food. Just behind him stood two servants with the tribal chieftain Abram between them.

Tahlahl stepped out and quickly took Babak by the arm and said kindly, "Babak, he's changed his mind. He's not hungry after all. Let me help you get this back to the kitchen."

He took Babak's arm firmly and dragged him away from the doorway. As he walked away, he saw Huni graciously invite Abram into his chamber, the look of fawning deference on his pharaoh's face entirely false to his nature.

The Scriptures tell us that God often sits in the heavens and laughs at man's machinations, his feeble attempts to supplant the Creator of all worlds on His own throne. We can imagine the Sovereign's chuckle now, can't we? The best advice available to Huni was to get rid of Babak in order to preserve his power base.

We have to ask, what power base? Unknown to this tiny pharaoh was that God was already working His own will in order to create a nation for Himself, and He was using Huni, His created being, to do it.

Sometimes we must laugh right along with God—especially when we look back at our own histories and see the struggles we put ourselves through as we tried to make our own will work. We laugh as we realize, despite our manipulations, we have ended up right where God wanted us all along, either prostrate before our Judge or on our knees in worship before our Redeemer.

Hagar was on her way to meeting this God, and it was her own "all-powerful" father who would place her on the path that would intersect with His.

"Girls!" their mistress remonstrated. "Please quiet down now—your revered father is coming. He is even now at the door." Sabah grasped two of the smallest girls firmly by their shoulders and jerked them around to stand at attention.

Hagar and her sisters immediately stopped their raucous play and lined up according to their ages. Hagar was somewhere in the middle of the thirteen children. A visit from the pharaoh, their father, was a rare occurrence; he spent much more time with his nine sons than he did with his daughters. Still, they were not without their value. A well-made marital alliance with neighboring kings and princes was a benefit not to be discounted.

Hagar was twelve years old, almost old enough to be contracted. She anticipated with eagerness the prospect of marrying a wealthy prince or even a king. Her little-girl imagination took her to palaces and gardens, with hundreds of servants at her beck and call and a swooning prince at her feet.

Perhaps today her father had come to single her out with the glorious news!

As the children stood waiting, eyes downcast as they'd been taught, silent—except for a stray giggle or two from the younger ones—Hagar knew they all had the same thought. Father, the all-powerful god of Egypt, was paying a visit. It could only mean one of them would be leaving. And Hagar knew each of the older ones hoped it would be her turn—such an event had come to four other daughters before this day.

Hagar knew she wasn't the prettiest of the lot, but she was healthy; her skin and eyes were clear, she was strong, and she was intelligent. Of all the remaining daughters, she worked the hardest at her lessons. Often, she was asked to teach the younger ones, something in which she took great pride. And she was fully a woman now—she'd started her monthly discourse, which proved she could bear children. The fact that she wasn't beautiful distressed her at times, but her other desirable attributes cheered her. Hagar waited in excited optimism—*surely it's my turn!*

Finally, the door opened with great ceremony and father walked in with his powerful stride, his closest advisers at his side. His robes swirled around his feet as he brushed by Sabah with barely a nod for his first wife. Twinkling golden lights played upon the walls, floor, and ceiling, reflected from the heavy jewelry around his head and neck. Hagar was distracted, watching the beautiful display of power. Distracted, that is, until he stopped in front of them, surveying his daughters, now completely silent and frozen in place. His eyes traveled over them one by one. He slowly walked from one end of the line to the other, stooping down to gaze into each pair of eyes and then stepping back to stare. Smoothing hair, opening mouths to inspect teeth, pinching arms. He seldom looked pleased with them, and today was no exception. He wore a sour expression, which had been stamped upon his face the moment the foreign woman, Sarai, had been sent back to her husband a few days ago. His chief vizier had mysteriously disappeared soon after.

Hagar almost felt pity for her father—almost.

Really! Hagar thought. *The way he leers at us is obscene. It's the same thing over and over, like we're his prize camels or something.* She immediately chastised herself for her rebellious thoughts. She was old enough to comprehend her value to the pharaoh of Egypt, and her unruly thoughts would certainly get her nowhere.

Father now halted in front of her, staring at her, letting his eyes slip from her hair, to her eyes, down to her developing bosom, stopping at her hips. She blushed under his gaze, thought she would die of embarrassment as his hands cupped her hips and gripped her thighs.

As her father moved down the line to younger and younger daughters, his eyes strayed her way again and again. Each time, her heart leaped. When he reached the end, actually patting the youngest on the top of her curly hair, he stopped and stared back at Hagar. Striding swiftly to her, he stopped again, stared, eyes measuring. Hagar kept her eyes demurely pointed at the floor, just barely able to see his face through her eyelashes. His expression was blank.

He stepped back and nodded at the five men with him. "Her," he said without explanation. He turned and marched out, his advisers trailing behind him.

Hagar couldn't contain herself any longer. As soon as the door shut behind him, she laughed out loud with delight. "Me!" she shouted in glee. "Me!"

Her sisters crowded around to congratulate her. Sabah clapped her hands loudly to get their attention.

"Children! Girls! Stop this nonsense immediately! I must prepare your chosen sister to meet her new family. Go to your lessons." Sabah then motioned to two of her handmaidens to follow her.

Hagar couldn't stop chattering as her mistress and the servants led her to the bathing room.

"Do you know his name, mistress? Have you seen him? Is he very rich? How far will I be traveling?" Her questions went unanswered. Perhaps Sabah didn't know the answers, which was odd, because she always had answers and was never shy about sharing them.

The handmaidens applied lotions, perfumes, and rare spices to her skin. *Surely, not a prince but a king had paid the dowry price!* she thought. She was, however, surprised at the quality of the clothes in which she was dressed. Not the worst, but not the best either. She'd thought she would wear Egypt's finest silks to meet her husband. *But no matter*, she thought. *I can't very well parade around the desert in fine silks. Perhaps I'll receive the finest clothes of* his *country!*

Her heart went on and on, wildly weaving a perfect picture of her new life soon to begin. As she was soaped and scrubbed, it was as if her existence here in the palace of the Egyptian god, her own father, was washed away. And as her hair and body were redressed, her new life was put on. Her exhilaration spilled out of her, causing Sabah to look at her with annoyance.

"Girl, will you please be still!" she admonished. Her grip on Hagar's arm made her wince in pain.

With courage and dignity born out of her new position, Hagar said proudly, "In a little while, *Sabah*, I'll be elevated above even your status. You'd be wise to not bruise me."

Sabah smiled at her knowingly as she dropped the new tunic over Hagar's head, clearly uncaring that Hagar had rudely called her by her given name.

"Surprises are indeed in store for you, my little princess. Be sure you are ready for them" was all her mistress said. Then with Sabah and the handmaidens flanking her, she was taken to a palace room where her father waited.

Her father didn't even look at her. He signaled her and her escorts to follow him. His stride was fast and heavy as he led the way to where she would meet her new husband.

For the first time, Hagar had a moment of misgiving. *Why are we going down the back stairway? Why does Father not look happy? Why won't he look at me, let me walk by his side, hold my hand as he gives me away?*

The agonizing thoughts swirled in young Hagar's mind. She tried to shove these dark questions aside and focus her thoughts on her glorious future, but her doubts mushroomed as she was led outside the palace into the hot, dusty afternoon.

There was no royal reception awaiting them—only a bedraggled older man looking like he'd walked over seven deserts. With him were three other men. That was all.

What is this? There should be a party, a celebration at her coming marriage to a prince or a king – not this secretive handing over of her to a group of filthy looking strangers!

***

Later that night, wedged between four of her sisters on their bed, plush with hangings from foreign traders, Hagar wept in shame and anger. Her girlish dreams of marriage to the swooning prince had become a nightmare. She had become not the wife of a foreign king or prince but the property of an elderly desert chieftain, who would, on the morrow, take her away from all she knew to live as a slave in a filthy tent in the desert. Never again would she play and gossip with her sisters, sit in the place of royalty in her father's palace, or dream of being the cherished wife of a prince. She finally fell asleep with the comfortless arms of her sisters around her.

The next day Hagar left with the strange foreigners. No one saw her off. No loving arms wrapped around her to wish her well in her new life. No dowry was given for her by her new master. In fact, Hagar was told that her father had *paid* the desert people to take her! Her father and her sisters weren't even there—only Sabah and two servants to carry Hagar's meager belongings. Sabah wouldn't even look at her as Hagar was unceremoniously handed over. She wasn't allowed to take her Egyptian finery, her personal trinkets, not even her gods. She had a sleeping mat and two changes of clothes—servant's attire.

She was to be the slave of the chieftain's wife, the woman, Sarai. As Hagar trudged away from the glamorous palace of

Memphis, where she'd lived from the moment she was born, she was as miserable as any child could be. But no one cared. Her life was turning to dust as dry as the desert floor.

The only kindness Hagar saw was in Sarai's watchful eyes. They hadn't spoken, but as Hagar stumbled along behind Sarai, carrying her own sleeping mat and Sarai's, she noticed Sarai's frequent backward glances.

Is that pity? I don't need your pity!

Hagar remembered Sarai's words. *We all have need of refuge. Who is yours?* It seemed Sarai had been right after all. She felt the hot tears spilling again.

Sarai was indeed correct. The need for refuge is universal on planet earth.

Refuge is a beautiful word. It means a place to hide, shelter, protection from danger or trouble, a place to find aid, relief, a place to escape.

Hagar was young—only twelve—and at that age, under normal circumstances, it's hard to feel the need for refuge. She was the daughter of the pharaoh, living a life of rank and privilege—albeit due to her usefulness to her father's political ambitions—so it seemed to her that *refuge* was something she was already living in, protected by the might of her father.

But life turns on a dime. One day Hagar was living a sheltered life in her father's *harim,* and the next she was trudging into the harsh wilderness, a slave with no shelter, no rights, no possessions, and no future.

Has your life turned on a dime?

One moment your life is following a predictable, almost boring path, and the next you're free-falling into the unknown. You're doing life the way you've been doing it for years, and suddenly all that is familiar is gone. You experience the unexpected: loss of spouse, loss of job, loss of child. Perhaps you experience loss of friendship—that beloved friend you have known from childhood betrays you. Or loss of health as you listen to the impassive doctor across the room explaining the disease—in incomprehensible words—that has invaded your body and to which you will slowly and painfully succumb.

These two are universal among humanity: experiencing loss and the need for refuge. It doesn't matter whether we admit our need for refuge or not—it is a fact.

Arrogance keeps us from realizing our need. We can live our entire lives never feeling the need for this place to escape, this need for protection, *refuge*. Or we seek it everywhere but where it can best be found. Wealth, possessions, talent, and human relationships are a poor substitute for the refuge to be found in Jesus Christ.

But then at that last moment, with the last breath, as earthly light dims, we know the truth. At journey's end, as we walk from this room to the next, the need for refuge looms, and we either have it in God, or we don't.

Hagar will discover there is no place but One to find refuge.

Hagar's eyes shone with anticipation. As she listened to Sarai explain the contract, her mind was busy once again building a new life for herself. She would no longer be a helpless slave, unable to rise above that circumstance. It wouldn't matter anymore that she was a hated Egyptian, that she didn't worship their god, that their language was difficult. And if she could just fulfill this contract, her future was assured.

She tried to keep her jubilant thoughts from escaping under her eyelids as she kept her face downturned. Sarai kept explaining, kept jabbering. In her excitement, Hagar was unable to comprehend most of the words. But she did decipher the words *child* and *son* – and the word *barren*.

Finally, Sarai asked, "Do you understand, Hagar? You must fulfill your duty to me in this request. Do you understand, child?"

Hagar bristled at the word *child*. She wasn't a child anymore. She was a full-grown woman. And she was very glad now that she had rebuffed the attentions of the young Israelite men who occasionally looked her way.

Cautiously, Hagar raised her eyes to meet Sarai's, trying to keep her mistress from seeing the triumphant gleam. The effort almost defeated her.

"Yes, mistress," she said. Hagar contrived to look innocent, even afraid. "Yes, I understand. I must bear Abram a son in your stead, because you are infertile."

A vicious slap across her face almost knocked Hagar to the ground.

"Never say that to me again, slave!" Sarai whispered ferociously.

That night she was taken to Abram's arms, and there Hagar found the kindness and solace missing in her young life since the day her father had cast her away. Abram was gentle with her, and Hagar felt she'd found her swooning prince at last in this elderly desert chieftain. He wasn't what she'd longed for, but he offered her security—if she could bear him a son, that security would be assured.

It wasn't many more weeks before she could tell Abram and Sarai she was with child. The glow of satisfaction in Abram's eyes was a balm to Hagar's spirits. At last she would have a home of her own, a child to cherish, and a husband who loved her.

She ignored the fleeting look of jealousy on Sarai's face.

***

Hagar ran. Pregnant, her belly just beginning to show, she couldn't run very fast, but nevertheless, she ran—her tangled black hair streaming behind her, her ragged tunic flapping around her legs, her tattered sandals slapping the hard desert floor. The landscape was harsh, unforgiving. She fell and got up again, scraping her legs and her palms on the hot sand.

She had no idea where she was going—just away, away from her beloved Abram, away from his shrew of a wife, away, once again, from everything she'd ever dreamed.

She sobbed as she ran. Abram had spoken to her of his God as they'd lain together. Many times he'd told her of God's love and care for him, journeying all the way from Ur. He'd told her of his protection and guidance. She didn't really care about his God though. Her Egyptian gods were quite enough to deal with. All she'd cared about was producing a child for him, a son, which would assure her place in his family line. Abram was rich and would take care of her. He was her only hope, her only refuge.

Hagar wasn't sorry about the way she'd treated Sarai. Sarai always lorded it over her anyway, treating her as if she were a harlot who'd stolen Abram right from under her nose. Sarai had evidently forgotten that the contract had been *her own* idea in order to produce a child. And then when she'd fulfilled that contract, Sarai's jealousy knew no bounds. And Hagar wasted no opportunity to remind Sarai that she, the little Egyptian slave, was the one who held Abram's heart because of the son she would one day place in his arms.

Hagar felt Sarai didn't deserve the blessing of children. But now, her own situation was grim.

She stopped to rest beside a spring of water on the road to Shur and to decide exactly where she was going. She longed to go back to Egypt to see her father—if she couldn't stay with Abram—but the journey was long. She shaded her eyes and looked south. *I'll never make it across the desert of Shur by myself.*

As she sat there, misery enveloping her mind, she cried out to her gods to either kill her or save her. Her soul was heavy, heavy with foreboding, dread, anger at where the road from Egypt had brought her.

She went over and over in her mind that scene she'd witnessed—hiding behind the tent folds—between Abram and

Sarai, the bitter words seeding her soul with a bitterness of its own.

"This is all your fault, husband!" Sarai had accused Abram. "I put her into your arms legally, as I'm under contract to produce an heir for you. I had no choice but to give her to you. But now that she's with child, you hardly look at me. *Her* comfort and well-being is all you think about now. And I see the way you look at her!" Sarai had begun to sob. "And now she, my own maidservant, treats me with utter contempt!" Sarai beat Abram's chest with her small fists as she spewed out her anger. "Mark my words, husband! The Lord will reveal who's wrong—you or me!"

Hagar smiled then from her hiding place. Sarai was finally on her knees, realizing who held Abram's heart. Hagar tenderly caressed her belly, thanking whatever god had caused the heir to seed and grow within her.

Abram's next words wiped the smile from her face and crushed the hope in her heart.

"Look. She belongs to you, not to me!"

How the bile had risen to her throat at that harsh pronouncement! She still tasted the bitter hatred.

"Deal with her as you see fit, Sarai. The slave means nothing to me."

Hagar had stiffened at the word *slave*. She peered around the curtain, caught Abram as he caressed Sarai's face, kissed the top of her head. She saw the gloat spreading across Sarai's face, her shining eyes looking up into Abram's as he gathered her tenderly into his arms.

It took all of Hagar's carefully built self-control not to launch herself at both of them and scratch out their eyes. She couldn't watch anymore as Abram stroked Sarai's back, soothing her anger, murmuring words of love to her. She drew back quietly and slipped out of the tent into the midday glare, hot tears of shame slipping down her cheeks—shame at her own foolishness to believe Abram would cast Sarai aside for her.

Oh, damn them! she thought. *Damn them!*

And Sarai had taken Abram at his word. It was as if Sarai was trying to beat the child out of her. Every infraction, no matter how small, was worthy of the rod across her back. Every mute, pleading gaze in Abram's direction brought a vicious backhanded slap from her mistress, every episode of the sickness a reason to withhold food from her. Abram did nothing. Hagar thought she would die of humiliation as even he looked at her with disgust as she doubled over outside the tent and retched the contents of her stomach onto the hard desert floor.

Where was this god of his now? Was she, Hagar, not worthy of his notice, his care, his protection? As she sat there beside the spring of water, the bitter misery washing through her, hands cupping her swollen belly, she despaired. She begged whatever god there was to be merciful to her and the child and kill them both.

Her mind gave way to grief. Desperate thoughts swirled through her head. *Can I kill the child before birth?* Her eyes roamed over the barren landscape looking for a stick, a twig, any instrument with which to root the child out. There was nothing. *Can I bash my head with a rock?* Again, not even a small rock to be had. She raged at that unmerciful god, spewing her hatred of him in her mind. Finally her thoughts quieted as she gazed drearily at the empty desert.

Hagar let her mind drift back to her life in Memphis. Her memories blew gently across her mind like the breeze swirling the sand at her feet.

She pictured her father striding about his palace followed by a cohort of subservient advisers. She saw him sitting astride his favorite camel, silhouetted against the bright desert sun, surveying his city. She remembered a time when he let her sit on the camel in front of him as he inspected his army—how proud she was that day! Surely she was his favorite daughter. Her sisters had envied her, and she'd taken every opportunity to remind them of her status. She recalled the pomp and ceremony that accompanied him on every visit to the *harim*—

she and her sisters dressed in their finery, lined up in front of him as he strode purposefully, eyes traveling over them as when he inspected his army.

And when Father had smiled at her, the sun came out.

Why, oh why did Father throw me away? And why do you throw me away now? Am I so unholy in my need of a husband and son that you cast me out? Out of my husband's home, out of the fellowship of the camp, out of the presence of whatever mercy there is in this life? And then you don't even give me tools to end my despair! Abram is a fool to worship you; surely you are the most capricious of gods.

Hagar bowed her head to the ground, slipping from the mound on which she sat to lie in the sand, her body and mind numb with heartache. The slow death that awaited her did not frighten her; it was the slow death of her unborn that made her mad with agony. The prospect was enough to kill her then and there. She lay there, unmoving, hearing the call of the jackal in the distance, feeling the hot desert breeze drift over her, lifting her hair. She no longer cared what happened next. Closing her eyes, she gave herself to whatever this god had decreed for her.

And in that moment, lying there in the mounting desert heat, unable even to lift her hand to get water from the spring, she felt her child move for the first time. The grief took her afresh. She wailed again at the sky, tears pouring out of her eyes, watering the ground on which she lay. And when she had spent herself again, she waited silently for death.

***

Hours later she awoke. So quietly that at first she thought it was the wind, the whisper drifted to her ears. She strained to hear.

Ha-Agar, the wind said.

No, not the wind. The waning light of the sunset brightened around her.

Sarai's servant, where have you come from, and where are you going?

Who was this? Hagar sat up and looked around, expecting to see the owner of the voice on the wind. There was no one, except the brightening of the light around her and a sweetness in the desert air.

My mind is gone. My grief has driven me mad.

The child within her moved again, somehow sending her thoughts down a new path. Hope grew in her heart. Perhaps Abram's god had finally heard her! Perhaps—*but if it is a god who speaks to me, why does it know my name but not what has happened to me or where I come from or where I am going?*

Hagar did the only thing she could think to do. She answered the voice.

"I'm running away from my mistress, Sarai," she replied through cracked, heat-swollen lips. The voice didn't ask any more questions, didn't ask why she was running away.

And with the next words, a glowing, indistinct form took shape before her, stooping to take her hand and lift her up. Her eyes refused to focus on the form, so bright with colors never seen on earth. She kept her eyes averted as she allowed the being to bring her to her feet.

Return to your mistress, and submit to her authority. I will give you more descendants than you can count. You are now pregnant and will give birth to a son. You are to name him Yishma-El, which means *God hears,* for the Lord has heard your cry of distress.

Somehow, with those words, belief washed over Hagar. She chose, in that moment, to believe the voice. She didn't know where that certain knowledge came from, but she *knew* this was the God that Abram had spoken of so many times. Abram had told her his God had no name, but she now named him.

She spoke the words back to him now. "You are El-roi, the God who sees me!" she declared in triumph. "Have I truly seen El-roi?"

And the God who saw Hagar gave her strength to stand, drink from the spring, and begin the journey back to the arms of her husband, Abram. This God of his would surely help her to withstand the jealousy of Sarai, and her son would be the father of a nation.

Hagar rejoiced as her steps turned toward home. With each step taken in the direction God told her to go, her confidence mounted. Surely, he was a God who both saw and heard. Surely she'd found refuge—not in her father, not in her husband, but in El-roi.

> The Lord looks down from heaven and sees the whole human race.
> From His throne He observes all who live on the earth.
> He made their hearts, so He understands everything they do.
> But the Lord watches over those who fear Him, those who rely on His unfailing love.
> He rescues them from death and keeps them alive in times of famine.
> We put our hope in the Lord. He is our help and our shield.
> In Him our hearts rejoice, for we trust in His holy name.
> Let your unfailing love surround us, Lord, for our hope is in You alone.
> (Psalm 33:13–15; 18–22)

There is much more to Hagar's story. She returned to Abram and submitted to Sarai's authority as God commanded. Difficult as that must have been, she had encountered El-roi, and the simple knowledge that she was seen by Abram's God carried her through the hard times of slavery, holding second place in her husband's heart, and living in a foreign land.

She gave birth to Abram's son, Ishmael, who held first place in her husband's heart for many years. She was there when Abram became Abraham and Sarai was renamed Sarah, and Sarah was promised her own son by the same angel of God who'd spoken to Hagar, albeit this time in human form. She witnessed Abraham's rescue of his nephew, Lot, and the destruction of Sodom and Gomorrah. And what must have gone through Hagar's mind when she learned that Abraham deceived Abimelech in the same way he'd deceived her own father?

There are many Jewish legends about Hagar's life. One, in the Midrash—a compilation of rabbinical interpretations of the Torah—quotes her thus, "It is better to be a slave in Sarah's house than a princess in my own."

Many scholars believe that after Sarah's death, Isaac went to find Hagar where she had traveled after being sent away with Ishmael, and brought her back to Abraham. Many believe that Abraham's second wife, Keturah—which means "tied to"—was indeed Hagar and that she had never married again. Some describe her as a virtuous woman who had adopted belief in Abraham's God and as "a woman of humility and piety. Indeed, few others were privileged to have an angel of G d speak to them twice, and produce miracles for them" (from the Midrash, www.chabad.org).

And God kept His promise to Hagar, making Ishmael the father of a great nation, one that still exists today. And the other half of God's promise is still true today, that there would always be strife between the families of Ishmael and Isaac.

You might be wondering what all this means to us in this century—the century of watching television on our phones, automated cars, drones, instant messaging, and social media. The century of wars fought with buttons and joysticks, gender confusion, and media-owned politics. On the surface, Hagar's life so many centuries ago has little resemblance to our own—except for the fact that El-roi saw her. As He sees every detail of your life from birth to death and beyond.

Have you met "the God who sees me"? It doesn't matter your circumstances, be they smooth and merry or rough and painful. El-roi watches you, longs for you—His beloved. Hagar's hard experience left her desperate and destitute. Yours may not be like hers, but it's no less wrenching—destitute emotionally and spiritually, desperate for peace, for love and acceptance, for reconciliation and forgiveness.

And if your life is proceeding smoothly, successes piling up around your feet, coming triumphantly through the tragedies, give God the glory and know that there will come another day for you—a time when you will need refuge from the evil in this age of death in which we live. When you find yourself there, be sure you incline your heart to El-roi, as Hagar did, and seek the only true refuge to be found, at His feet.

Father, may we flee to You in times of desperation and times of joy.
We believe You are the only place of refuge to be found.

Study Questions—The God Who Sees Me

1. Consider a time when you needed refuge. What were the circumstances?
2. Where did you go to find refuge?
3. Have you ever been alone and destitute, as Hagar was? Is that time now? Where will you turn?
4. Have you now met El-roi? Has He changed your circumstances? If not, how has your thinking changed since meeting "the God Who sees me"?
5. If your present circumstances are running smoothly and successfully, is your need for El-roi the same as when your life was upside down and desperate?

Chapter 2
The Scarlet Rope

Now listen! Today I am giving you a choice between life and death, between prosperity and disaster.
—Deuteronomy 30:15

"Have you heard, sister? They say they're coming—those strange people who worship only one god," Ahlai said. The inn was full of carousing travelers as it usually was in the early evening.

"Shhh!" Rahab warned, a finger to her lips. "Yes, I've heard, but we must talk later, not here." Ahlai acquiesced to her older sister's admonishment and fell silent.

The two women continued to work, cleaning tables, making small talk, serving wine and food to the weary travelers who frequented the house in the wall. The other women who worked at the establishment could be seen leading some of the men, from time to time, up the stone steps to the rooms overhead, where the real money was made.

Rahab had been to those rooms. Since coming to Jericho when she was young, she'd worked in this inn and now managed it for the absent owner, who lived northeast, in Gilgal. Once she was well established, she'd brought her family to live in Jericho from the Amorite hill country to the east. Her aged parents, brothers, and other relatives lived on the other side of town, kept by her steady work.

Now, in her position, she did not have to go to those rooms, and she'd managed, so far, to keep her young sister out of them. For that, she was grateful.

There was another reason she was grateful. The owner rarely

presented himself. As long as the money flowed his direction, he was happy to leave the running of the inn to her.

As she worked, quickly turning tables over for whoever would occupy them next, she watched Ahlai serve two men sitting by themselves at the outer edge of the room. They looked and behaved differently from the other travelers, evidenced by their respectful treatment of her sister. Rahab wondered who they were and what they were talking to Ahlai about so intently. Rahab decided she must ask for an explanation later. Sometimes Ahlai, at the tender age of twelve, could be quite naive.

She turned her attention to one of her harlots coming down the stairs, a man in tow. She breathed a sigh of relief, seeing no bruises on her face and that she was smiling. Rahab was protective of her women—she would tolerate no abuse of them. If there was an incident, if any of her women were mistreated, she had a strict policy: the man was never allowed back to her establishment. The inn's popularity in Jericho and the surrounding region was her protection—abuses were rare because no one wanted to be barred from it.

Rahab deplored the darker aspects of her life. When she was brought here, from the eastern lands where she was born, she was barely eleven years old. She'd been put to work in the home of a leading tradesman at the time, a brute of a man who made his living buying flax from the farmers who lived in the outlying areas. He'd buy it cheap and sell it to the linen makers at an exorbitant price, making himself rich and unpopular. He drove her unmercifully, making her work into the night, helping to sort and pile the flax bundles. During the day, she was at his beck and call, cleaning his home and running errands while he sat, his bulk barely able to fit on a stool. She learned subservience quickly—and the consequences should she fail, if he detected the least rebellion in her usually downcast eyes.

Rahab thought it a mercy when he was finally murdered—no doubt by one of the farmers he cheated—and his apprentice took over the business. He was a fairly young man and kinder to her. Fifteen by then, she had learned much about the running of the flax business just from observation. The new owner realized this and appointed her the apprentice's apprentice. Instead of long hours in the field sorting the flax, he'd hired two young boys to do that work. He brought her out of the fields to help him, and working side by side, the business slowly prospered again. The farmers who sold the flax to them gradually realized they were being treated fairly, and soon more business than they could handle poured in.

Alas, good times never last long. Within a year, the new owner took a wife, and jealously judging Rahab too comely to work closely with her new husband, she threw Rahab out on her ear to get along as best she could. For a time, she lived on the streets of Jericho, begging food and sleeping in alleys.

Finally, a kind woman brought her to the inn, cleaned her up, fed her, and let her sleep on a real sleeping mat instead of the hard floor. She was left alone for several days. But then the woman brought her to one of the upper rooms for a serious talk. Rahab was told she'd need to begin earning her keep. She was put to work in the kitchens at first, helping to clean pots. She'd gradually earned the right to help with food preparation, and then moved up to actually serving the food to guests.

Rahab found that she enjoyed the work, the interaction with travelers, listening on the sly to their tales. And she seemed to be a sought-after server—some actually asked for *her* to serve them—but she didn't get the significance of that until months later.

She was heartlessly introduced one day to the real business of the inn—which she'd tried to put out of her mind—when a traveler who'd been there before requested her to serve him and his three companions. She obliged and was soon listening with rapt attention to an exciting tale of being set upon by a group of six robbers and how they'd escaped, killing them all. The color was high in her cheeks, eyes alight at the drama; the speculative looks on the men's faces went unnoticed.

Later, gathering the cups and plates from their table, she

noticed the same man at the stairway, money changing hands between her rescuer—the kind woman—and himself. She watched nervously as the man drunkenly came her way. Reaching her side, she was aghast when he suddenly bent down, picked her up, and threw her slight body over his shoulder, her long hair brushing the floor. Yelling for his comrades to follow, he carried her, struggling and crying up the stairs. After that day, her wages increased, but the cost to her was high.

Rahab sighed, all of these memories flooding back to her as she watched Ahlai. Yes, she deplored the rooms upstairs, and she'd do anything to save Ahlai from them, but she couldn't do anything about what happened up there to all of the other young women. She had a business to run—it was the way of things in Jericho. She must keep reminding herself to be grateful that someone else had to engage in that sordidness and not Ahlai—or herself anymore.

Life is hard. And the gods we worship seem not to care. Hastily, she retracted that rebellious thought, unwilling to take the chance that one of those gods might actually be listening.

***

Later that night, after closing and locking the doors, Rahab made her way up the stairs to the small quarters she shared with Ahlai. She walked by each of the six other rooms, looking in, making sure her women slept alone. Travelers were not allowed to spend the entire night in the rooms—the girls needed their rest. The rooms on the other side of the house accommodated the guests. Or they could spend the night in the street. Rahab didn't really care, as long as there was no trouble.

Coming into her room, she was surprised to see Ahlai still wide awake. Usually the young girl was fast asleep by this time of night. And not only was she still awake, she was excited about something.

"At last you are here, sister!" she exclaimed, hopping up from her sleeping mat.

"Shhh, keep your voice down," Rahab admonished. "Why aren't you sleeping? It's late, and you must be up early, or have you forgotten?"

"Oh, I couldn't sleep," Ahlai said, now whispering.

"And why is that?"

Ahlai sidled closer to Rahab, who was straightening the room, moving restlessly, wishing Ahlai was asleep. Ahlai laid a hand on her arm.

"Did you see the two travelers I served tonight?"

Rahab stared at her. "Well, which one, little sister? Could you narrow it down for me? I saw you serve at least twenty travelers tonight!"

"I guess you're right," Ahlai replied with a sheepish giggle. "The ones sitting nearest the door, to the right of it. Those two. They didn't stay very long—they said they had business in the town and just came for dinner." She added, "You needn't worry—they were very polite."

Rahab stopped fussing with the linen, which was stored in a small closet in their room, and turned to face Ahlai.

"Well, what about them? Why has their visit excited you so?"

Ahlai put her lips next to Rahab's ear and whispered, "They're very strange. They spoke to each other in a strange dialect—one which I barely understood—about their leader. They didn't ever say his name, but I could tell they were talking about some plan or other. And they used the name of a god I've never heard of."

Ahlai drew back and looked into Rahab's face. They stared at each other for a moment. Rahab finally broke the silence.

"What god?" she asked casually.

"I can't pronounce it, and they whispered it. It was almost as if they didn't want to say its name out loud. It was very strange," Ahlai said.

Rahab looked down, smoothing her gown, then reached up to her hair, winding a lock around one finger—a sure sign she was thinking deeply.

Ahlai waited, anticipation clearly building.

Rahab looked into her sister's eager face and came to a decision. "Well, it's nothing to do with us, Ahlai," she said briskly. "Now, it's time you were in bed asleep instead of making up silly intrigues where there are none. Off with you—go to sleep."

Disappointed, Ahlai did what she was told. Rahab knew she hadn't heard the end of it from Ahlai, but it was time they were in bed. Ahlai lay down, and as usual, Rahab tucked the thin blanket around her and kissed her on the forehead.

"No more storytelling," she said severely, but softened it with a smile.

Rahab then lay down on her mat, staring at the ceiling. Now *she* was wide awake, wondering about the two travelers. *What business would they have in Jericho? Who was the god they'd spoken of? Who was their leader? What plan?*

Rahab tossed and turned, questions bombarding her, and then finally decided the only way to satisfy her curiosity—which she really couldn't explain—would be to talk to the two travelers herself. She would seek them out tomorrow if she could and lay all of this to rest.

Ahlai probably invented at least half of this tale anyway!

From this inauspicious beginning, Rahab the harlot will be transformed into Rahab the rescued, earning a place in the lineage of David and of Christ Himself. Her story is fairly familiar, found in Joshua, chapters two through six. She's also mentioned in Hebrews 11:31, Matthew 1:5, and James 2:25.

Her story is one of danger, intrigue, and espionage—worthy of any modern Hollywood motion picture. I wonder, though, how Hollywood would treat her. I suspect they'd focus more on the sordid aspects of her life in Jericho—after all, ratings are important.

Would Hollywood ignore the clear fact that the God of Israel was busy in her life—unknown to her—setting the stage for her to make the most important decision of her life? That she would soon be faced with a choice, a choice that would determine the path she'd walk for the rest of her life? A choice between life or death?

Would they try to understand, and communicate to the audience, the curious question *why—why* did she help the Israelite spies? Would they clue in to the possibility that God, her Creator, had created the questions in her life so He could answer them for her—that He'd created the stage on which she stood in order to enter her life at just the right time?

Would Hollywood be drawn to the inevitable conclusion that the sovereign God of the universe passionately pursued this insignificant, immoral, second-class citizen of Jericho, marking her for His own, as He unfolded His stupendously large agenda in her life? I highly doubt it.

Yet, that is exactly where we must go to understand the significance of her story to our own stories.

So settle down and strap in for a wild ride—but as you hang on for dear life, don't forget to ask yourself, *where does her story intersect my own? What is God's stupendously large agenda in my life?*

Early the next day, just before dawn, Rahab put one of her more responsible serving girls in charge of the inn for a little while. There wouldn't be any business for several hours anyway; the place didn't really come alive until about midday.

She went out into the street, looking for the two travelers, perhaps bedded down in an alley. The sun was just making its appearance as she walked leisurely up and down the narrow walkways and the main thoroughfare as she surveyed the shops just coming to life. There weren't many people about yet. Those who were, were feeding animals and preparing for the business of the day. Several small children ran about, having, no doubt, escaped their parents in favor of a little freedom before *their* chores must begin.

Rahab saw no evidence of the travelers. She casually asked a few people but received no information. She retraced her steps, looking for any sign of them. Nothing. Disappointed, she turned around and headed back to the inn. Perhaps they'd gone back to wherever they'd come from. *It's just as well. Now I can tell Ahlai they're gone, and she'll stop making up adventurous tales about them.*

She entered the dining area, noting the cleanliness and orderliness. It soothed her. Rahab didn't enjoy chaos; she was fond of her smoothly run inn, the predictableness, the lack of any surprises. There was always the occasional scuffle over money or women, but Rahab quelled those with a firm hand, garnering the respect of her patrons. And from her point of view, those who made trouble need not be patrons. Looking around, she savored the peace of the moment.

If only I didn't have to engage the upstairs rooms, I'd be completely happy with my life. But you have to take the bad with the good, I guess.

Rahab shook herself out of her reverie and went upstairs to wake Ahlai. The sun was now above the horizon. Ahlai should be up by now, but her late night coupled with her vivid imagination caused her to sleep in.

I'll soon nip this nonsense in the bud!

***

Abir awoke suddenly. Stiff and uncomfortable from sleeping on the ground all night, he sat up and stretched in the early dawn. Rubbing his eyes, he looked around for his brother, Tobiah. The place where he had lain was empty, his cloak in a heap. Abir felt the cloak—cold. He must have been gone for some time.

Worried, Abir jumped up and ran to the small hill and up its side, where he could view the gates of the city. In the distance, he could see someone stealthily approaching, outlined against the shine of the waning moon—now just a sliver behind the surrounding hills. He stared for a moment, thinking it was Tobiah, but he couldn't tell at this distance. Considering it might be an enemy, Abir dropped into a crouch behind the hill and waited, listening for the man's footsteps. *I can take him if he doesn't have a weapon. And where's Tobiah?*

Crouching there, trying to decide if he should move farther down the hill or not—and berating Tobiah for disappearing—he suddenly heard the faintest of footfalls on the other side of the small rise. Knowing the element of surprise was in his favor, he waited another moment and then stood and charged up the hill. Halting at the crest, he looked this way and that and saw nothing. He scratched his head, confused—then was brutally knocked off his feet, rolling down the hill, arms and legs tangled in the body of his attacker. He tried in vain to break their fall, but he couldn't while trying to protect himself from his unknown assailant. Abir knew he must gain control of the situation if he was to live through it.

They finally came to a dusty halt at the bottom of the hill next to their camp. He quickly rolled away from the other man and jumped to his feet in a fighting stance. His attacker lay motionless on the ground about five feet from him, face in the dirt. Abir, nursing a severely bruised knee and various scrapes and cuts, nevertheless took a cautious step toward him.

"Stand up and fight like a man!" Abir commanded with all the bravery he could muster. *If I get out of this alive, I'm going to kill Tobiah for leaving me!*

The man's shoulders shook, his face still turned away. *He's crying?*

That thought gave Abir courage, so he stepped to the man's side and roughly rolled him over. The sun now peeped over the horizon, directly into Tobiah's face—not crying, but laughing—with tears streaming down his cheeks. He jumped up and assumed a mock fighting stance, fists in front of him.

"Abir, if you could just see your face!" he said to his brother, hardly able to get the words out. "You look like...like..."

Tobiah gave up the attempt at speech and sat down hard on the ground, laughing uncontrollably at his older brother.

Abir's expression changed from confusion to anger. He rushed his brother, who clearly had not noticed his mood change. Abir fell on top of Tobiah, yelling at him, pummeling him with his fists. Gaining the upper hand, he rolled Tobiah over onto his back, and sitting astride him, he gathered two fistfuls of dirt and ground it into Tobiah's face. Coughing, Tobiah begged him to stop.

"I'm sorry, brother! I'm sorry I laughed at you! Please stop!" Tobiah struggled to get the words out, but it was almost impossible with the dirt in his mouth and nose and Abir's strong hands around his neck.

The brothers were no strangers to this—they'd been sparring most of their lives—but the underlying love, comradeship, and common goals formed a foundation that protected them from actually hurting each other. They had always been the best of friends and would gladly have died for each other. This time was no different. Abir was angry, but he had no wish to hurt Tobiah.

Abir stood up abruptly with a final kick in Tobiah's direction, causing another cloud of dust to settle over the younger boy. Abir limped a few feet away, his back to Tobiah, trying to get control of himself. He knew his anger was based on fear for their safety in this foreign territory and would dissipate eventually, but he didn't want Tobiah to think all was forgiven and forgotten too soon. *He needs to learn a lesson, and I'm going to be his teacher.*

He heard movement behind him and turned around, fully expecting Tobiah to continue the scuffle. Instead, he saw him standing a few feet away with tears in his eyes—and not tears of laughter.

"Abir, I'm sorry. I saw you pop up behind the hill and crouch down again, and I just couldn't resist..." Tobiah started and then stopped at Abir's severe expression. "Brother, are you badly hurt? You're limping."

"Continue," Abir said. "Explain this foolish play, when we're sent here by Joshua on serious business."

"But I was just practicing what you taught me," Tobiah began weakly, clearly trying to persuade his brother he was rehearsing the strategies he'd been taught, instead of indulging in boyish war games.

"I saw you tuck down behind the hill. I knew you waited for me to come closer, and that you would ambush me when I was close enough. So instead of coming straight at you, as soon as I judged you would charge—and actually you made a lot of noise when you stood up again—I went wide and dropped down the other side to the right of you. I was right behind you when you crested the hill. It worked perfectly, didn't it, brother?" Tobiah concluded.

Abir saw the eager expression and didn't have the heart to berate Tobiah for his irresponsibility. After all, he was barely a grown man, still with childishness in his heart.

"Yes, it did work well, my young scoundrel," he finally said, coming closer and clapping Tobiah on the shoulder.

Tobiah breathed a sigh of relief.

"But where were you? Why did you sneak away?" Abir asked, not willing to completely let him off the hook.

"I decided to go back to the city gates and see if there were any early risers about who could give us any information," Tobiah answered.

"And?" Abir asked. "Were there?"

"No, I didn't talk to anyone. The gates were shut, but I managed to scale the wall in a weak place where it had some footholds. I peeked over, but there was no one about except for that innkeeper walking up and down the streets. But I didn't go into the city. I decided I'd better wait for you," he finished, looking at Abir expectantly.

"You did well not to go back in yet. You'd hardly have looked innocent, climbing the wall to get in," Abir said gravely.

"You're right, brother, as usual, and I was wrong," Tobiah said shamefacedly. "But," he added with a grin, "it was great fun!"

"You young rascal! What am I going to do with you?" Abir exclaimed.

"Now *that's* something I've never heard from your lips before—ha! I've been hearing that ever since we joined with Joshua's army. Admit it, brother. I have the makings of a fine soldier!"

"You do have the makings of a soldier, Tobiah, if we can just keep you alive long enough, considering your rash exploits. And today's no different," Abir said, gripping his brother's shoulders and shaking him a little.

"Now come, Tobiah. We must remove all trace of our camp, pack up, and go back into the city. I've been thinking, unlike you," Abir said.

"Thinking?" Tobiah picked up his cloak.

Abir, using his own cloak, swept over the dirt, erasing their footprints and the evidence of their sleeping bodies.

"Yes, thinking." He broke off in exasperation. "Tobiah, you left your coin bag over there—go get it, you young fool!" Abir commanded.

Tobiah quickly obeyed, tucking the coin bag into the lining of his cloak.

Abir, satisfied with his work, motioned they should leave.

"Well, what were you thinking?" Tobiah asked.

Abir walked slightly behind Tobiah, using his cloak to brush away their dusty footprints and the evidence of their frantic roll down the hill. As they crested the top and started down the other side, he shook his cloak and put it on. There was no need for such caution on this side of the hill, marked with many footprints from townspeople and travelers.

"I think we must enlist an ally in the town," Abir said quietly.

"An ally!" Tobiah exclaimed.

"Shhh! Don't talk so loudly—voices carry over this valley."

"Okay, I forgot. But wouldn't enlisting an ally be dangerous? What if—"

"Yes, of course it's dangerous. We must be very careful

whom we choose. It must be someone who knows people, has heard things." He paused. "I was thinking. Do you remember that young serving wench from the inn? She'd be in a position to hear gossip, war stories, what people are saying. What do you think of her, Tobiah?" Abir watched his brother closely, waiting for his answer. *Let's see if he thinks clearly on this question.*

Tobiah considered carefully. They were approaching the gates of the city, so he stopped for a moment.

"Well, Abir, I don't think so. She's awfully young, and you know how young girls are—hardly able to keep a secret. For instance, think about our young cousin Abigail. She chatters all the time, and I don't think she even knows what she's saying half of the time. I judge that serving girl and Abigail are about the same age." Tobiah looked expectantly at Abir.

"Excellent!" Abir said, clapping his brother on the shoulder. "You decided well—those were my thoughts exactly."

Tobiah smiled broadly, clearly happy he'd finally made Abir proud.

"Now, what about the innkeeper? Remember, the serving girl told us she's her sister. What about her?" Abir continued his testing of Tobiah. *I'll make a spy of him yet!*

This time Tobiah answered more quickly.

"We'll have to test the waters there, brother. We haven't even spoken to her. We'll have to figure out a way to meet privately with her."

"Yes," Abir agreed. "And most important of all, we must ask God to give us a sign that she is the one we can trust or if it's another." Abir glanced around at the empty landscape and then at the city gates, now opened to allow traders and travelers in. Abir noted the contingent of soldiers idly standing by the gates. *Not so idle,* he thought. Their gazes casually roamed over Abir and his brother, and Abir knew their presence had been noted and their descriptions would be remembered.

"Let's go," Abir said, waving Tobiah forward. He turned his steps again toward Jericho, Tobiah following.

***

Rahab was uncaring in the face of her younger sister's grumbling attitude at being awakened.

"The inn won't run itself, Ahlai," she admonished. "Now, I need you to get down to the kitchen and begin preparations for today's guests."

Her tone brooked no dissent, and Ahlai obeyed immediately.

Rahab had to admit to a certain tiredness herself, with her late night and early rising. *I hope today will be quiet,* she thought as she set their sleeping quarters to rights before making her way downstairs. She peeked into each room on her way down, making sure her girls were in their beds. She let them sleep on—they would not be needed in the tavern until later. Looking at each young face, brows cleared of stress during sleep, she shook her head. *They're all so young. They should be at home with their parents, innocent, playing with friends. I wish...* But Rahab couldn't finish the thought. She must get on with the business of the day.

She went downstairs and set the eating and drinking area to rights, making sure all would be ready for the day's business, clearing the plank that served as a bar and making sure the jugs behind the bar were full of ale.

When Rahab inspected the work in the kitchen, she found Ahlai washing the last of the tankards from yesterday and stacking them up to be carried to the bar. The cook Rahab employed, her first cousin, was preparing to go to the market to buy goat meat and vegetables to make Rahab's popular stew. She patted Ahlai on the back as she stepped past her to the back room.

Rahab climbed the stairs leading to the roof of the establishment. As she reached the roof, the stiff breeze blew her hair into her eyes. Hurriedly, she inspected her drying flax, laid out in a sheltered corner of the roof. Rahab had added this little side business a few years back to augment her income, taking care to keep her profits secret. She didn't want to share even this small amount with the inn's owner. She placed stones on the drying flax to keep it from lifting in the wind.

After finishing, she looked out over the countryside. From her vantage point on the city wall, she could see for miles. She often came up here for solitude, away from the carousing in the inn. As she looked out over the dry landscape, she could see a caravan in the distance, approaching Jericho. *There must be thirty camels! I wonder who it is.*

Rahab hurried down the stairs—she must prepare the cook to buy more than usual at market and let the serving girls know the inn would be busier than usual today. *So much for an easier day!*

After notifying the cook and handing him more coin, Rahab organized the serving girls and then ran back up the stairs to the roof. Shading her eyes, looking north at the caravan, she spied a familiar litter in the midst of the camels. *The owner of the inn is paying a visit!*

Rahab was surprised but not concerned. The inn turned a nice profit, and she kept it in good order. But she and Ahlai would be sharing a room with one of the serving girls this night—Manasses always took over their room when he visited. He refused to sleep in the larger quarters where men were entertained, so as not to sully himself—he himself never indulged in those pleasures when visiting Jericho. And he refused to sleep in the guest quarters on the other side of the inn—he wanted paying guests there. So he forced Rahab and Ahlai to give up their room to him. Rahab sighed. *At least the inn was clean and prepared for business – that should make Manasses happy.*

Rahab marched down the stairs and into the kitchen, beckoning to Ahlai as she strode into the bar area.

"Ahlai, Manasses is just arriving. I want you to go up to our room and clear out our things and tidy the room—he will want to sleep there tonight. You can put our things in little Mary's room."

Her sister's shoulders drooped.

"It's all right, Ahlai. It will most likely be for this one night only," she said kindly. "Now go. They'll be here soon, and I'll need you down here."

Ahlai trudged up the stairs.

Rahab had two of her serving girls help her push four of the largest tables together to form one big one for Manasses and his men. She judged, based upon the last visit, there would be about twelve to fifteen hungry men to feed. His lowlier servants could eat out on the street. She took a last look around the room, satisfied to note it was orderly and swept clean, tankards stacked up on the bar and ready to be filled with ale.

Hearing shouts in the street, she smoothed her clothing, tucked a stray hair behind her ear, and stepped to the front door to greet her special guests.

***

As she unlocked the door and opened it, she was pushed back by two young men who fell into the room, almost at her feet. Grabbing at a table, she managed to keep herself from falling to the floor. They sprawled facedown for just a moment and then hurriedly stood up and faced her. Rahab was astonished to see they were the same young men Ahlai had spoken of and whom she, Rahab, had gone out to look for earlier this morning.

"We're not open yet, sirs. You'll have to come back later," she told them firmly. She started for the door to show them out but was halted by a hand on her arm. Surprised, she looked at the man who gripped her firmly. She tried to shake him off, but he held on.

"Good woman, we would speak with you—just for a moment. My name is Abir, and this is my brother, Tobiah," he said in a dialect Rahab could not place. She held his gaze for a moment, then came to a decision, pushing her intense curiosity aside for the moment.

"Sir, I don't have time. Do you see that caravan arriving? That is my master, the owner of this inn come to visit from the region of Gilgal. Now, let go of me—I must go out and greet him," Rahab said, finally jerking free of him.

"My apologies. We meant no disrespect...uh, what is your name?"

"This is my establishment," she said, refusing to answer his question.

"We meant no disrespect, mistress. We'll be staying a day or so longer and will come back when it's more convenient. We hope—my brother and I—for a chance to speak with you," Abir said politely.

"Yes, well, we'll see. I really have to go," she said, peering out the door and seeing Manasses's litter being settled.

Tobiah found his tongue and said, "Yes, we want some of that wonderful stew we had last night. Will there be any this night?"

Rahab's voice softened. "Yes, I'm sure there will be," she said, amused by the look of anticipation on his young face. "Now, please leave, and I may be able to spare you a little time later. Please come back at midday," she said, gesturing to the door.

Rahab stood at the entrance and watched them walk leisurely down the street. They were deep in conversation, the young one occasionally waving his hands excitedly.

They seem harmless enough. And that younger one...he's just a little older than Ahlai. I wonder what they want with me?

She recalled what Ahlai had said about their strange god—were they of the people who worshiped only one god?—and that they'd seemed to discuss some plan. *What's it all about?*

The voice of Manasses called her back to the present.

"My dear Mistress Rahab! How nice to see you!" He bowed in front of her.

Rahab stood with lowered eyes, bowing courteously to him.

He reached out and grasped her chin, raising her head. "Come...come, my dear! No need for all this ceremony between friends."

He ran a practiced eye over her and Ahlai, who'd appeared

in the doorway and was standing just behind Rahab.

"You're looking well, Rahab," he said, peering around her at Ahlai.

Feigning astonishment, he exclaimed, "And who is this? No, it can't be—not young Ahlai—so grown up! Come closer, my dear. Let me get a better look at you."

Ahlai moved shyly up to Rahab's side. She started to take another step forward, but Rahab grasped her sister's arm, staying her where she was.

Manasses reached out and cupped Ahlai's face gently, speculation in his eyes. Rahab reacted without thinking. She slapped Manasses's hand away from her sister but then was immediately dismayed at her hasty action.

"Forgive me, sir," she said quickly to cover her rude behavior. "She's just gotten over the fever," she explained, pinching Ahlai to silence, "and I would hate to see you contract it."

Manasses took a step backward, bumping into a servant behind him. He leaned down, grabbed a handful of dirt, and vigorously rubbed it into his hands. Then wiping his hands on the servant's robes, he turned back to the two women.

"My thanks to you for the warning, Mistress Rahab. And where has she been sleeping while she had this mysterious fever? Not in the room I'm to occupy, I trust?"

"Oh, I made her sleep on a mat up on the roof, sir. I didn't want it to be passed to any of our guests," Rahab answered, now wishing she'd never embarked on this fabrication. *I should have just told him to keep his filthy hands off her!*

"Very wise. Well, I'm just staying for one night, possibly two, but I'd like to inspect everything as usual," he said, "particularly the books. Are they in order?"

"Indeed they are, sir, as is everything else. Please come in and get settled while your servants unload your bags," Rahab said. "Will you be needing someone to tend to your camels?"

"No, no, my young men will do that." Turning to said young men, he commanded, "Take the beasts to the outskirts, and stay out there with them. I'll see food is brought to you. And those of you who've never experienced Mistress Rahab's stew, you're in for a treat!"

Rahab and Ahlai ushered the company of men into the inn. Rahab saw questions in her sister's eyes, but she hushed her with a finger to her lips.

"Later" was all she said.

***

"Sister," Ahlai whispered. "You lied!"

They'd retreated to a small alcove off the kitchen where supplies were kept.

Tears shone in the girl's eyes, and Rahab pulled her close. She could hear Manasses, who'd gone upstairs with his men, noisily getting settled. As no one lingered nearby, she took this opportunity to explain.

"Ahlai, you're only twelve, and—"

Ahlai drew away from her and laid her hand gently over Rahab's mouth. "No. Don't say it," she said. "Thank you, sister." They exchanged a long look in which all of the sad and weary years flowed between them.

So Ahlai understands what happens in those rooms. Well, she's growing up. It's time she knew.

"Ahlai," she said, drawing her sister close again. "You must understand. If I could, I would close those upstairs rooms. They represent what's evil in this world."

Ahlai nodded her understanding. Still, Rahab wanted her to know the truth.

"Ahlai, what happens up there is not love—not the kind of love our father has for our mother. What happens in those rooms is taking—of innocence. That's why I lied. I couldn't bear to let you go to them, do you hear? I've been dreading this day for years. Manasses has been biding his time, waiting for you to grow up. It seems he thinks you're ready now to become…to become—and I can't bear the thought, my little one. I'll die before I let him have his way in this."

Rahab's emotion got the better of her. She stood silent for a moment, trying to control the tears building up behind her eyes. Ahlai reached out and took her sister's hand, bringing it to her own face, tenderly brushing it across her cheek.

"I know, *Rahab*," Ahlai said softly, using her given name, as between equals. "I know."

Rahab drew her into her arms, hugging her tightly. It seemed that Ahlai had suddenly, in the last few moments, grown up and they were truly equals. *No, allies. We're allies now. Instead of Ahlai needing all the protection, we'll protect each other.*

It was a good feeling.

Sisters are a beautiful thing. *Webster* defines the relationship several ways—one being *a biological female relative*—but I like this one: *a female friend or protector regarded as a sister.*

Women naturally bond from the heart; men bond intellectually. Women not only share interests but feelings and emotions. Men can be very close—hence the term *blood brothers*—but their closeness is based upon something other than emotion, usually loyalty or perhaps a shared skill.

Female relationships, because they're based upon emotion and heart bonding, can suffer more traumatic breaks than their male counterparts. Of course, men can suffer betrayal and hurt feelings, but most men seem able to either bounce back into friendship or just walk away from the relationship, moving on more effortlessly than women.

And those women who have biological sisters with whom they share close ties are most fortunate. Not only do they share the female bond, but they share a family history.

I say all this because I had a sister once. In my first book in this series, *Who Are These People? Spiritual Lessons Learned in Obscurity*, I briefly talk about my sister's death and how it affected my family. But there is more to the story.

Holly, a young wife and the mother of two small boys, took her own life at the age of thirty-one. I still remember the call we received at my parents' home, gathered there at the request of my brother-in-law. I remember his voice starkly telling me, with my parents on the extension, that my only sister had shot herself. That she'd driven all the way to Missoula, Montana, and checked into a motel, gun hidden in the back of her vehicle.

I can still hear the drop of the phone in the other room as my mother and father collapsed in grief. I still turn to see them, in the dim light of their bedroom, holding each other. I see the stricken faces of my children as it sank in that they'd never see their beloved Aunt Holly again.

The universe shifted that day. It had shifted five years earlier when my younger brother, Scott, was killed in a car accident. But that was an accident—this was deliberate.

Sisters are supposed to know each other's hearts, each other's griefs, each other's pain. Sisters are supposed to talk to each other for hours, spilling their thoughts to each other. And we'd done that. I felt I could say anything to Holly and she would still love me. Even though she was three years younger than me, I looked up to her—she had a quality of loving and caring for others that I didn't have. It still seems curious to me, even after almost three decades, to use past-tense verbs when speaking of Holly.

A few weeks before her death, I'd called her, telling her I'd be in Bellevue, Washington, for a conference. She eagerly suggested we meet at the coffee shop in the hotel where I'd be staying. She'd have to drive from Monroe, Washington, a distance of about twenty-six miles, but she wanted to, so of course I agreed.

At the end of the conference, I loaded my bags into my car and drove home—completely forgetting my date with Holly. She called me that night and asked, "Where were you? I waited all afternoon in that coffee shop."

Of course, I was apologetic, making the excuse of being so tired that I forgot.

I asked, "What did you want to talk about?"

She answered, "Oh, it's not really important. I've got to get dinner going now. Bye!"

How could I have known those would be the last words I would ever hear Holly say? The guilt I felt—still feel—will never be completely washed away in this life. Would she have told me her pain? Would I have been able to help her, to prevent what happened that March in 1989? Would I have been able to protect her from the attack of an enemy too strong for her to fight?

Where were you? I waited for you…

I can picture her today, clearly, sitting in that coffee shop for hours, watching out the window for my car to pull in, drowning in her secret sorrow. I sit across from her, trying to read her face as she sips her coffee, picks at her napkin nervously, glances out the window again—sad eyes drifting over the parking lot. Her thoughts shout at me.

You promised you'd come. I need you – I'm in trouble and I need you. Where are you, sister? Why aren't you here?

I felt like an accomplice in her suicide for a long time. I failed to protect her from a morass of pain that ended with the blast of a gun in a faraway motel room. I blame myself for being too preoccupied with self to even remember the arrangements I'd made with her.

A decade or so later, my husband, my father, and I stood in the parking lot of the very motel where she'd ended her life. We walked in the front door. I looked around, waiting. We walked back out the door. As we reached our car, I looked back one more time, searching.

What were we expecting? Holly to suddenly walk out the front door of the motel and join us in the parking lot? An explanation? And for me, absolution? Forgiveness for not showing up that day? Holly, why aren't you here? I wasn't there for you then, but I'm here now.

The only sound was the wind.

"She's not here," I said.

Still we stood, three islands in the midst of a sea of people talking, laughing, making plans, and uncaring that we stood waiting for time to roll back to yesterday when life was understandable, when things made sense.

"No," Dad finally said. "She's not, I guess." We got back into our car and drove away.

Don't waste time. You never know when you'll have that last conversation with someone you love.

Much later, during the early evening dinner hour, Rahab wandered out of the kitchen to see Ahlai deep in conversation with the two young men she'd spoken to yesterday and who'd fallen in the door at Rahab's feet earlier today. Ahlai was animated, clearly enjoying the discussion—Rahab could see her eyes shining even from a distance.

Rahab motioned to her, and Ahlai broke off the conversation, threading her way through the tables to Rahab's side.

"And what was that all about, Ahlai? You look as if secrets were being told."

"No, no, sister, we were just renewing our acquaintance from yesterday. They're very interesting travelers. Do you have time to come and meet them?" She added hesitantly, "They asked to meet you."

Rahab gazed suspiciously in their direction and then made up her mind. She wanted to know what nonsense filled Ahlai's mind.

As she approached them, they stood. Rahab was not impressed with their appearance. They had dirt and bruises on their faces, as if they'd been in a scuffle. And neither had bathed recently—but that was common among her guests.

But their expressions caught her attention, especially the older one. He looked at her politely, his eyes staring directly into hers, unwavering. He bowed to her slightly, never taking his eyes from her face. Rahab judged his look to be free of the typical speculation she encountered at the inn. It was a measuring look, but not accompanied by the customary leer. The young one simply looked innocent—not yet a man, not yet burdened by the normal needs of men.

The two young men exchanged a glance and a slight nod. Rahab's curiosity mounted. *What are these two about?*

"Welcome to my house," she said with a polite curtsy. "If I can be of service, please let me know."

"Thank you, mistress..." The older one spoke.

"My name is Rahab," she answered.

"Thank you, Mistress Rahab. My name is Abir, and this young rogue is my brother, Tobiah."

"And I believe you've met my sister, Ahlai. I hope she has been serving you well during your stay in Jericho," Rahab said and then added pointedly, "And what brings you here, may I ask?"

"We're looking for—" Tobiah began eagerly.

"Flax—we're flax buyers," Abir interrupted smoothly.

Rahab noted his hand firmly gripping his brother's arm. Her eyes narrowed with suspicion. *What had the young one been about to say?*

"We wondered if there's somewhere we could speak in private," Abir said with a wave of his hand, "away from this rabble."

"About flax?" Rahab asked pointedly.

"Well—yes."

Ahlai, standing beside Rahab and clearly confused, stammered, "But...but, you said—"

Rahab cut her off. "Yes, we can speak privately. Come back later tonight. My sister and I will be waiting."

"No disrespect to your sister, but we prefer to meet with you alone," Abir said firmly.

Rahab saw Ahlai's disappointed expression. She placed her arm around her sister and said, equally firm, "Whatever you must speak to me, you can say to Ahlai. We're...*allies.*"

Joy blew across Ahlai's face, and Abir acquiesced

immediately.

"As you wish, Mistress Rahab."

Rahab turned to go but was held by Abir's hand on her arm.

"Yes? Is there something else, sir?"

"Well, we, my brother and I, we..." Abir stopped, a curious expression, unreadable, on his face. Rahab was piqued—she was unused to the inability to read the expression on a man's face.

"Yes?" She gently removed his hand from her arm.

Abir's expression cleared, whatever thought he'd had obviously gone from his mind.

With an open-hearted grin, he said, "We were wondering if you're serving that excellent stew tonight."

Rahab chuckled. *I'm beginning to like these two!* "Yes, we are, sir. Ahlai, see that they have their fill—and it's on the house."

"Thank you, mistress. Your kindness is overwhelming and unexpected. We look forward to our meeting later tonight," Abir said gravely.

Rahab nodded, dropped a swift curtsy, and strode away, leaving Ahlai to minister to them. Rahab needed a place to think, so she headed to the roof.

***

Ahlai served them each two large helpings of stew, accompanied by bread and ale, and then left them alone. After eating, they refilled their tankards and sat back to talk.

"Brother," Abir began in a low voice, "tell me your thoughts about Mistress Rahab and her young sister."

Tobiah thought for a moment. "I like them," he said. "And I believe we are directed by God to speak to them—although I'm a novice at hearing such clear direction. But we prayed for direction, and here we sit, basking in her kindness. Is that not direction?" Tobiah waited respectfully, clearly gratified to see his brother's slow nod of assent.

"I have another question for you, Tobiah. What were you going to say when I interrupted you and fabricated that story about being flax farmers?" Abir's gaze burned Tobiah's face, his expression now turned down in shame.

"I…I guess I got ahead of myself. I was going to say we're looking for an ally in Jericho, someone who could help us complete our mission."

Abir allowed his severe expression to soften.

"It was stupid, brother, and I'm glad you stopped me. I have a lot to learn," Tobiah finished ruefully.

"Well said, Tobiah," Abir replied softly. "I thought something of the kind. You were ready to tell her the truth, but I wanted to be sure of her." Abir stopped abruptly, looking at Ahlai, who was pouring ale for a large group of men.

"Isn't it interesting that we're looking for an ally in Jericho, and then Mistress Rahab uses the exact same word when talking about her sister…here, what's this?" Abir suddenly stood, sending his stool crashing to the floor.

Tobiah then saw what Abir saw and was immediately on his feet.

Ahlai was being roughly passed from one man to another at the large table. The men grabbed at her, pulling her hair and her clothing. One grasped at her bosom while slobbering all over her neck. Another then shoved her into the lap of the man at the head of the table. Tobiah made a sudden move toward them, Abir just barely holding him back.

"Wait," Abir hissed into his ear. "Wait, you young hothead!"

Everyone in the inn engaged in the drama, clapping and catcalling, egging the men on in their abuse of the young girl. As she landed in the leader's lap, his large hands grasped her around the waist as his lips went to her neck. She struggled, finally twisting around and viciously slapping his face. He grasped her shoulders and planted a hard kiss on her lips. Ahlai now sobbed openly, struggling mightily to get away from him. His grip only tightened.

Drawing back from her, eyes glittering, he said in a voice clearly audible to everyone, "Here, mistress, we're going to have to teach you your manners!"

Standing up, arm still around her waist, he shouted to the crowd, "What do you think? Shall we teach her some manners?" The crowd broke into applause. Some of his men stood to their feet drunkenly, reaching for Ahlai, who was almost swooning in the man's grasp.

He turned toward the stairs, dragging Ahlai with him. "Well, come on then! You'll all get a turn with this young one!"

He strode to the stairway, gripping the frightened girl—pathetic in her fright—as his men followed after, reaching for her hair, her skirts, her bodice, touching her, their faces clearly betraying their evil intent.

Into this chaos and clamor, Abir's voice boomed out over the noisy inn.

"Unhand that young woman, sir! At once!" He strode through the tables, kicking stools out of his way and pushing patrons aside. Reaching Ahlai's side, he roughly grabbed the shoulder of the man. Tobiah was right behind him. The crowd quieted, shocked into silence.

"What business is this of yours?" said the man with his hands on Ahlai—his friends called him "Manasses"—slurring his words. "This is my establishment!"

"And she is *my* business, sir!" Abir said with a snarl. "Let go of her!"

"Oh, I see." Manasses sneered. "You want first taste. Well, that's okay with me, you young jackanapes. Take her! But pay me first," he said, his hand out.

He'd let go of Ahlai, who fled into the kitchen. Manasses laughed uproariously.

"I guess now you'll have to chase that one. I wish you well of her," Manasses said, still with his hand out.

Abir reached into his cloak and brought out a coin, laying it in the odious man's hand. The hand was not withdrawn, so Abir laid two more coins in his hand. Satisfied, Manasses went back to his table, followed by his men, yelling for more ale.

Abir, breathing hard at the foot of the stairs, wondered if they should leave. He caught Tobiah's glance, aimed behind him at the kitchen door. Tobiah nodded discreetly. Abir looked and just caught Rahab as she beckoned to them from the kitchen, then disappeared behind the door. He turned back and surveyed the crowd. They were deep into their tankards, some already passed out on the floor. Manasses, along with his men, paid them no mind. Abir gestured to Tobiah, and they walked unobserved through the kitchen door.

***

Abir just caught the whisk of Rahab's skirt lifting up the stairway at the back of the kitchen. He and Tobiah followed, arriving at the roof just behind her.

She had gone to Ahlai, who was sitting on a parapet, sobbing. Rahab held her tightly, her eyes shiny with tears. They approached and stopped a few respectful feet away, the two women silhouetted against a bright full moon.

Ahlai finally stopped crying, calmed in the arms of her sister. Ahlai clung to her, face buried in Rahab's shoulder as she gently murmured soothing words.

Tobiah shifted, obviously uncomfortable with the emotional scene and unfamiliar with this kind of grieving. Abir gave him a warning glance, motioning him to stand still and wait.

At last the sisters stilled. Rahab looked up at them and began to say something, but Ahlai came alive at that moment. Launching herself at Abir, she fell in a heap at his feet, clutching at his legs.

"Oh, sir," she said in a strangled whisper, "thank you. Thank you! How can I ever repay you?" She wept afresh.

Tobiah leaned down and patted her head awkwardly. He said nothing—but his gesture seemed to calm the girl.

"Mistress Ahlai," Abir said gently, "there's no need for repayment. That man and his friends are repulsive and no gentlemen. We couldn't stand by and let that happen. Anyone would have done the same thing."

Rahab stood up and stretched out her hand. Abir took it in his firm grasp.

"No, sir, I don't think so. Most men in this town would have stood by awaiting their turn at her. I thank you from the bottom of my heart." Her words were spoken sincerely, her steady brown eyes fastened upon Abir's. She leaned down and helped Ahlai to her feet, moving a step back.

"And now, sirs," she said with a look from Tobiah to Abir, "what is your business in Jericho, and how can we—my sister and I—aid you?"

Abir looked up into the night sky and said, "Praise be to YHWH, who directs our steps and guides us into all truth."

She gazed at him with surprise and curiosity.

Abir said, "Mistress Rahab, are we quite safe up here to talk for a while? Is it likely we'll be interrupted?"

After a whispered exchange between the two women, Ahlai ran to the stairway opening and went down. Abir looked at Rahab, a question in his eyes.

"Just wait a moment. She'll be back shortly," she said.

Rahab walked over to the parapet, silently gazing out over the dark landscape, her back to them. She leaned over, both hands on the stonework as she wept softly. Tobiah started forward, but Abir rested a hand on his arm. Abir shook his head.

After just a moment, she turned around to face them.

"I know firsthand what you've saved Ahlai from," she said sadly but with great dignity, her eyes darkened with grief.

Abir nodded slowly, not knowing what to say to this woman who'd suffered so much and was now trying to protect her sister from the same suffering. Just then, before he could formulate a response, Ahlai reappeared, closing the door to the stairway softly behind her. She silently crept past Abir and Tobiah, stepping to Rahab's side. Another whispered exchange.

Rahab nodded, then turned to Abir.

"Ahlai has given instructions to my cook and his helper that we are not to be disturbed and has locked the kitchen door to the roof. So, gentlemen, we can speak privately and will not be interrupted. Now, how can we help you?" Rahab said.

Abir, now that the question was put to him again and he had the freedom to answer, didn't know where to start. Rahab seemed to understand.

"Just start at the beginning," she said gently.

And so he did.

Beginning with God's rescue of his people from Egypt, under the leadership of Moses, and ending with Moses's successor, Joshua, sending Abir and Tobiah to spy out this land—under the control of the pagan Amorite kings—Abir used the most persuasive words he could muster to help Rahab understand their mission.

***

Rahab listened carefully to Abir, her heart stirred beyond anything she'd ever experienced. The night wore on, under the bright moon, as the whispered conference continued. And when Abir's tale was finished, both Rahab and Ahlai sat back on the stone parapet, staring at these two men—once enemies—now, somehow, allies.

And here, Rahab is faced with her decision.

Would she believe these two spies, sent to destroy her city, backed by the one true God, of whom she'd never heard and had never seen? Would she see how God had brought her step by step to this moment? Would she understand that her hard life of subservience and slavery has been played out against the backdrop of a loving Creator whose hands had been busy, bringing her to this moment of decision?

And you—will you take a moment to consider *your* life—with all of your tragedies, losses, confusion, and betrayals, mixed with moments of joy—as sovereignly directed by the God of Israel, who never slumbers in His relentless pursuit of you?

He gently brings us to the point where we have nothing but

Him—no resources, no emotional reserves, no mental cleverness—and we must look upward to Him for rescue.

Rahab is there, at that point. Are you?

The next morning, Rahab was startled awake by a furious banging on the door of little Mary's room. She got up and opened it cautiously. Ahlai, clearly afraid, sat up on her mat, clutching at her blanket. Mary did not even stir, sleeping soundly.

It was only the cook.

"Mistress, the king's men are here and are demanding your presence," he said quietly. "I think you must come now."

"All right, tell them to wait—I'll be down as soon as I'm dressed," she responded. *Now what?*

She dressed and told Ahlai to wait in the room—on no account must she come down. Ahlai nodded, obviously relieved.

Rahab went to the door, then turned and said, "It'll be all right, little sister. I'll be right back."

She stopped in the kitchen, smoothed her hair, and took a deep breath. Opening the door to the dining area and bar, she was startled to not only see the king's men but Manasses and his men. She stepped slowly until she was standing right in front of them.

Looking at the leader of the king's men, she said in a steady voice, "How may I be of service?"

"We are sorry to disturb you, mistress, but some rumors have come to our ears," said the commander in a rough voice.

"Oh? And what rumors have come to your ears?"

Manasses broke in. "Now, Mistress Rahab, you know exactly what he's talking about," he began in an overbearing tone.

The commander quelled him with a fierce look.

"We have heard news about the barbarians who are said to

be moving this way from the east. It's said two of their spies are in this region and that they have been entertained here. What have you to say, mistress?"

Rahab didn't hesitate in the least. "Why, nothing, sir. I have nothing to say because I don't know who or what you're talking about," she said with great dignity. "Now, sir, if you'd care to, I can prepare some food for you and your men—*free of charge*, naturally—so you can be on your way." Rahab ignored the sound of disgust from Manasses at the words *free of charge*.

The commander's gaze at Rahab's unflinching face was hard and measuring. Then he seemed to make up his mind.

"Very well, mistress. You may prepare that food, and we will be on our way and continue our investigations. But," he added with severity, "we will be back. Perhaps then you will have the answers I seek, that your king seeks." He motioned to his men, and they marched out the door.

Manasses stepped to Rahab's side, putting his lips to her ear. "And I'll be back, too, Mistress Rahab, to watch the fun," he hissed. "Do not think I will easily forget what happened here last night at the hands of the men you *say* you know nothing about. I will see to it that they get what's coming to them. And your sister. That will be *quite* enjoyable."

Rahab stared at him, barely controlling her revulsion. She kept her face blank, choosing not to react to his vile words.

"You are, of course, welcome anytime, sir. After all, *you* are the owner here," Rahab said cordially, stepping away from Manasses. He threw her a look of disgust, and then he and his men left.

Rahab let out a sigh of relief. *I must step carefully. And I must protect those two young men.* She went back up to her room to reassure Ahlai that all was well for now, and to think.

***

That night, as previously arranged, Abir and Tobiah did not appear at the inn for supper. Rahab had gotten word to them that they must stay out of sight until after dark. She'd given instructions that they were to enter the back door of the kitchen from the outside—the cook would be waiting for them—and then they were to go to the roof and await her coming.

Manasses and his men arrived early for supper. They watched the preparations closely, clearly on the lookout for the two strangers. Rahab felt their eyes upon her as she served food and drink to her guests. Near the end of the long evening, Manasses called her over to their table.

"Why are you serving tonight, Mistress Rahab? Where's that luscious sister of yours?" he asked, gazing intently at her. Rahab flushed.

"She has fever again. I told her to stay in bed."

"Fever *again*. My, my. She must be a very sickly young woman," he said, then added with a grin at his companions, "But she seemed very fine last evening, right, boys?" His men laughed uproariously at the bad joke. Rahab made to move away but was suddenly gripped by Manasses's iron hand.

"Make no mistake—I'm watching you. And I *will* have her in those upstairs rooms one day soon. She'll make me a lot of coin."

Rahab jerked away from him and strode quickly to the kitchen door, unable to take any more. A fresh outbreak of laughter followed her.

As she entered the kitchen, her cook silently pointed up and nodded his head.

Good, they made it. I'll have to sneak up there soon – we have much to discuss.

As Rahab loaded more bowls of stew onto a tray to take out to her guests, she heard a commotion in the dining room. Setting the tray down, and after exchanging a worried glance with the cook, she went to the door and opened it a crack. The king's men were back—pulling stools out to sit at the table with Manasses.

"Quick. Go up and tell them to hide under the drying flax," she whispered to the cook.

He dropped his cutting knife and went up immediately.

Coming down again, he nodded at her.

She picked up her tray and went through the door into the noisy dining room, displaying a calm and a confidence she didn't feel.

"Ah, Mistress Rahab!" the commander said in a jovial voice. "We meet again. I'd like some of that stew I've heard about."

Rahab set a bowl in front of him and turned to serve another table.

"Give that tray to one of your serving wenches. I would speak with you. Now!" the commander barked.

"Sir, I'm unaccustomed to being given orders in my own establishment," she said bravely.

"My establishment, my dear," Manasses said severely. "And you will do as the commander asks, if you please."

Rahab knew she was defeated. She handed off the tray and turned back to the commander, standing quietly with hands folded in front of her, heart thumping wildly.

"I have it on good authority that the two spies have been seen in this house, Rahab," he said, dropping the courtesy of her title. "Now, where are they?" His tone was menacing, dripping with suspicion.

Rahab knew she'd need to tread carefully with this one.

"Yes, sir, I'd heard that. Another guest, just this evening, mentioned he'd seen the two strangers earlier, skulking around the city gate. He described them to me—low characters, practically illiterate, who could not give a good account of themselves." Rahab hoped to divert attention with this false description of Abir and Tobiah.

"So you have not served them here?"

Carefully, mixing a little truth into her lie, Rahab replied, "Not I, sir. I'm really not sure if they've actually been *here*."

One of Manasses's men spoke up then.

"We saw them, mistress. They were here, last night, brashly interfering with our business. And weren't you seen speaking with them?"

Careful, careful.

"Oh, *those* two! I'm not sure they're the same men you seek. Yes, those two were here and caused some kind of a ruckus—I'd heard that. But I didn't know who they were or where they were from. I was told they left Jericho at dusk, and good riddance to them. If you want, you could catch them if you hurry." She looked innocently at the commander. He gazed back at her for a long moment, then stood up quickly.

"All right, mistress, I'll bite," he said brusquely. To his men, who'd stood up with him, he said, "Let's go catch them."

As they trooped out, tightening their weapons around their waists, Rahab heard one of the soldiers ask a question—she couldn't hear the question—but she did hear the commander's answer.

"Alive would be better—we need to find out who they are and who sent them—but dead's all right. Whatever you have to do to obey the king's edict."

Rahab breathed a sigh of relief as she heard them moving off in the direction of the gates. They'd left the door open, so she closed it, standing a moment with her back to the room, gathering her composure.

She turned around to find Manasses's eyes boring into hers, his expression suspicious. She ignored him and went about her business, clearing a table and picking up litter left by the soldiers. She moved quietly, deliberately, his eyes following her around the room. Finally, after taking the dishes and litter to the kitchen, she came back into the dining room and approached him.

"Sir," she said with contrived respect, "it's late. I'd like to close now and get some sleep. And my girls need rest." She waited, eyes downcast, afraid he would read what was in them.

He stared at her, clearly turning things over in his mind.

"Yes, yes, my dear," he said, somewhat kindly.

False, false!

"And we'll be staying on tonight. My men and I will be heading back to Gilgal early in the morning. Please see that we are well provisioned for our journey."

The news could not be more welcome to Rahab. She tried to hide her relief.

"Yes, sir, I'd be happy to. I'll just go now and instruct my cook to arise early and begin preparations for you so that you can leave at first light. Thank you, sir," she said, trying not to sound too eager.

He stood up, gathering his cloak around him. As he passed Rahab, standing submissively before him, he stopped and leaned close to her face.

"If I were you, my dear, I'd come clean when those soldiers come back," he whispered in a fatherly tone. "I'll warrant you've never seen the inside of the king's prison, nor do you have any idea what use he and his soldiers find for young women there. I know you think I'm debauched, but you really don't know the meaning of the word."

Rahab's face drained of color as she stared at him wide-eyed.

Clearly satisfied, he took his leave of her.

Manasses and his men made their way upstairs. She followed them up, trying desperately to control her fear. She checked the rooms as she usually did. Her girls were asleep. She peeked into the room she and Ahlai had been sharing with Mary, but did not see her sister's form on her sleeping mat. Worried at first, she then surmised where Ahlai could be found.

Once more making sure there was nothing more Manasses needed for the night, Rahab hurried back down the stairs and out into the kitchen. She gave instructions to the cook, then proceeded up to the roof.

"Rahab, my cousin," whispered the cook.

Rahab stopped at the door.

"Be careful. You tread a thin path, but I'm with you."

His loyalty brought sudden tears to her eyes. "I will," she whispered back.

"Remember me and my family, Rahab," he said, pleading in his eyes. "I've heard stories about this god of the Hebrews. They say he dried up the Red Sea for them to cross. Which of our gods could do that?"

Rahab answered with a slow nod.

"Yes, my good friend, so have I heard these stories, long before these two arrived," she said. "I won't forget you."

***

She found, as she suspected, Ahlai deep in conversation with Abir and Tobiah. The two men stood respectfully as Rahab approached. Her mind was made up.

"Sir," she said to Abir, her eyes bright in the moonlight, "I know the Lord has given you this land. The talk is that everyone is afraid of you. Everyone is living in terror. For we have heard how the Lord made a dry path for you through the Red Sea when you left Egypt. And we know what you did to Sihon and Og, the two Amorite kings in the east, across the Jordan River, whose people you completely destroyed."

"Yes, Mistress Rahab, our God is the only God. Your people worship false gods, if I may be so bold as to say it. YHWH is the God of our fathers, Abraham, Isaac, and Jacob, the same who defeated the pharaoh of Egypt with the plagues and with the waters of the Red Sea," Abir said, and then, gently, "The same who is the creator of all, even your people, the Amorites."

"No wonder our hearts have melted in fear!" Rahab replied, her voice rising in passion. "No one has the courage to fight after hearing such things."

Rahab looked from Abir to Tobiah, noting the compassion in their eyes. Then her eyes met Ahlai's, her love for her sister rising in her chest, remembering the bravery of these two who had saved Ahlai from the evil intent of Manasses and his men. Warmth flooded her being as her heart melted in the presence of this God of whom they spoke, unknown to her until this moment.

"I believe…I believe," she stammered, her tear-filled voice clear and low. "The Lord your God is the supreme God of the heavens above and the earth below."

Abir grasped her hands tightly, his eyes now filling with tears. Tobiah looked heavenward, his lips moving. Ahlai clung to Rahab, whispering that she too believed.

Rahab gathered herself, knowing they weren't safe yet.

"Sirs, what is your objective in Jericho? You have gained an ally in my sister and me, but for what? We are only two women."

"Our God has given this city to us," Abir said.

Rahab blanched.

"What does that mean? I'm no soldier, but I know your people's reputation. Your God fights for you."

Very gently, Abir grasped Rahab's shoulders and, looking straight into her eyes, he said, "It means we will destroy every living thing in Jericho, mistress. We dare not leave anyone alive."

Rahab digested this information while Ahlai sobbed quietly beside her. Suddenly impatient with the younger girl, she turned and gripped her arm.

"Here, Ahlai, calm yourself! I must think." She walked away, keeping her back to them.

The velvet night blanketed them in silence as she gazed at the dark desert, her home since she was eleven years old. The enormity of Abir's words cut her soul to ribbons as she considered what she must now do. She must fall in with his plans, or she, Ahlai, and her whole family would be destroyed. Her new belief in their God steadied her as she turned to face them again.

"You must get away, now, tonight. You must not be caught," she said. She strode back to stand in front of Abir.

"Yes, I know. But I fear it will be harder getting out than it was getting in," Abir said with a wry grin.

"I will help you," Rahab replied.

Ahlai gasped next to her.

"But, sister, you heard what he said…how…why…would you help them?"

Rahab quelled her with a look.

"Yes, we will help you, but first I need some assurances," she said, ignoring Ahlai's confusion.

"Assurances?" Abir asked.

"Yes." She took a deep breath, hardly knowing how she had the temerity to ask such a large favor.

"Go on," Abir said with a glance at Tobiah. "I'll listen, and if I can grant it, I will."

Tobiah reacted with a nod of assent.

"Swear to me by the Lord that you will be kind to me and my family since I have helped you. Give me some guarantee that when Jericho is conquered, you will let me live, along with my father and mother, my brothers and sisters, and all their families."

Abir listened as Rahab brought out her request haltingly, his eyes softening at her clear devotion to her family. The silence stretched before he answered, the four of them standing closely together in the blackness of the night, lit only by the shining moon.

Rahab thought for a moment her request would be denied. *What will we do then?*

Finally he said, "Indeed, we offer our own lives as a guarantee for your safety. If you don't betray us, we will keep our promise and be kind to you when the Lord gives us the land. My brother, do you agree to this?" He looked at Tobiah.

Tobiah reached for Ahlai's hand, and taking it gently in his own, he said, "We will protect you and yours with our own bodies if need be." Ahlai nodded, keeping her hand in his a moment longer.

Rahab put her arm around her sister, hugging her tightly.

"And now," Rahab said, going to a large clay pot in the corner of the roof, "you must go." She reached into the pot and brought out a long rope made from the very flax she sold—dyed a brilliant scarlet color. The two men watched as she strode to an opening in the parapet nearest where they stood and secured the rope, letting the end of it dangle to the ground.

"Climb down and escape to the hill country. Hide there for three days from the king's men who search for you. Then when they have returned from their search—for they will come back here to question me further—you can go on your way."

Abir considered her plan and agreed to it.

"But," Abir said, "you must do your part, mistress. We will be bound by the oath we have taken only if you follow these instructions." He paused, waiting.

"Yes, we will follow your instructions, sir," Rahab said.

Abir fingered the rope. "Leave this scarlet rope hanging from this very opening. This rope is *our* means of escape. But," he went on, "it is also *yours*. When we come back into the land, all your family members—your father, mother, brothers, and all your relatives—must be here, inside your house. If they go out into the street and are killed, it will not be our fault. But if anyone lays a hand on your people inside this house marked by the scarlet cord, we will accept the responsibility for their death. If you betray us, however, we are not bound by this oath in any way."

Rahab drew herself up with dignity. "I accept your terms," she said, courage flooding her soul as she said the words.

And she sent them on their way, leaving the scarlet rope hanging from the opening.

A short time later, Israel came back to Jericho and laid waste to it in the most unusual battle ever recorded.

Abir and Tobiah did as instructed by Rahab and made it back to Joshua's camp. They were debriefed by their commander, telling Joshua and the other leaders all that had happened to them in Jericho.

"The Lord has given us the whole land," they said, "for all the people in the land are terrified of us."

That was all Joshua needed to hear. Early the next morning he led the Israelites to the banks of the Jordan River, and they prepared to cross over and take the land promised generations before to Abraham, Isaac, and Jacob by the God who always keeps His promises.

After preparations were made, and following God's instructions to the letter, the Israelite army crossed over—in a way reminiscent of the parting of the Red Sea for Moses—and marched toward Jericho. The fifth chapter of Joshua opens with all the Amorite and Canaanite kings west of the Jordan shaking in their sandals at rumors of the exploits of this tiny band of Israelites led by their powerful God. Those kings completely lost heart and "were paralyzed with fear because of them" (Joshua 5:1).

And then in accordance with God's instruction, all of the Israelite males were circumcised, a sign of the renewed covenant between God and His people. The men who were alive and had come through the wandering in the desert had never been circumcised, so this must be done before Israel moved in to conquer Jericho.

After this was completed, God said, "Today I have rolled away the shame of your slavery in Egypt" (Joshua 5:9).

All the while, in Jericho, what do we suppose was happening? As Rahab waited patiently for Israel to move in and conquer the city, what might have been going through her mind? Some time had gone by—perhaps a few weeks. Did she lose heart? Did she go to the roof each day and search the horizon for her rescue? Did she check to make sure the scarlet rope was still hanging? Did she touch it, thinking of Abir's words, "This is your rescue"?

Finally, the day came. Rahab, from her rooftop perch, saw them coming in the distance and rejoiced. She quickly gathered her family into the inn, which now became a place of refuge instead of a place of subservience and degradation.

The family waited behind the barred door. Rahab had checked the cord once again—it was in place. It remained only for them to wait.

What could have gone through Rahab's mind when, instead of hearing the advancing Israelite army storming the city gates and the sounds of battle and the cries of the dying, she heard the sound of marching feet circling Jericho. Did she leave her family waiting in the inn and go up to the roof to see what kind of battle this was? Was she disheartened or confused to see not a battle waged in which she and her family would be rescued, but a strange band of priests and warriors carrying rams' horns and a curious-looking box? Did she go back down to her family and tell what she'd seen?

And still they waited, questions circling their thoughts, unsure now why they waited. Would their rescue ever come? Did they whisper among themselves, wondering if Rahab had lost her mind to expect rescue from these warriors who didn't fight? They didn't understand what they were waiting for—this non-battle.

They waited six more days, cramped in the small inn. Perhaps some argued to leave. Did Rahab plead with them not to go outside?

"But," they might have said, "where is our rescue? Why is it so long in coming? Nothing's happening out there! Why can't we leave and go back to our lives?"

Can you picture this scene in your mind—the days of fear-filled waiting as their Rescuer, the God of Israel, tarried?

Of course we can picture it—because we also wait. We await our rescue from this mad, mad world in which we live. Do we lose heart? Are we confused, uncertain what kind of battle is being waged for our rescue? Do we, tired of this wait, want to go back—perhaps like Rahab's family—back to our "before" lives, when we did not suffer the disappointment of waiting; before our belief in this unseen Rescuer was ridiculed; before the Light shone in our hearts, illuminating our glorious future outside the cramped spaces of this evil world?

We can see the end of Rahab's story. The God of Israel came back to Jericho, leading Joshua and his army. The walls of Rahab's prison fell on the seventh day of waiting, just as Joshua was promised, and the city was taken. Only Rahab and her family were spared, just as Abir and Tobiah had promised her.

The Amorite woman who dared to believe the One over the

many gods of her people became a citizen of Israel, leaving the ruins of her former life for the newness and cleanness of her new life among God's people. She's hailed as an example of towering faith in the books of Hebrews and James.

But that's not all. In Matthew 1:5, she's named as the wife of the Israelite man Salmon, the father of Boaz—the same Boaz who married Ruth, the Moabite woman who traveled with Naomi to Israel. Rahab became Ruth's second mother-in-law—tying the books of Joshua and Ruth together in the great unfolding drama of redemption. There are other theories in rabbinical writings and legends about Rahab's later life—for instance, that she married Joshua—but I choose to believe what God's Word says about her. These other theories must not distract us from the theme of her story—rescue by the God of Israel.

Are you not encouraged by Rahab's final rescue? I am. She lived in a pagan city, had a miserable past, and worshiped false gods. Yet God in His infinite mercy relentlessly pursued her and won her, placing her strategically in the direct lineage of Jesus Christ. She was the great-great-grandmother of King David.

What a wonderful story of God's redeeming love!

Your story and mine are no less wonderful. We may not experience rescue from a human enemy, but rescue from the dominion of sin and Satan are even more miraculous. Every heart that's captured and conquered by His love makes the angels in heaven throw a party—a party that we will eventually join at our final rescue.

The words of God to Joshua, "Today I have rolled away the shame of your slavery in Egypt," are ours also. Jesus bled scarlet on the cross, died, and rolled away the stone at the tomb, removing our shame of sin and giving us newness of life in Him along with the promise of the coming final victory over this world.

As Rahab had to choose, so we must—life eternal or death eternal—one with the promise of God's presence forever, and

the other with the promise of God's absence forever.
Which do you choose?

Father, help me to choose rightly.

Study Questions — The Scarlet Rope

1. Is your life hard right now? Can you identify with Rahab, living in a world of degradation but not knowing that rescue can be yours?
2. Has God brought a rescuer into your life? Someone who has told you the Gospel story and has urged you to believe? Have you believed?
3. Can you recount a time in your life when God told you to do something that made no earthly sense? Did you obey or walk away? What was the result?
4. Do you have a family member or friend with whom you have become estranged? Have you considered the possibility that your last conversation with that person might be tomorrow? What is God asking you to do about that?
5. The *inn* where Rahab and her family waited for rescue is a microcosmic picture of the *world* in which believers today await their rescue. How many similarities can you name between the two?

Chapter 3
By Night

Jesus replied, "I tell you the truth, unless you are born again, you cannot see the Kingdom of God."
—John 3:3

"What say you, Nicodemus? Will you accompany us?"

Nicodemus, at least a head taller than the one who questioned him, looked around the small room off the temple courtyard, filtered sunlight illuminating the group of men gathered in the early morning. His searching gaze stopped on the grim face of his friend, Joseph. Nicodemus thought he could read Joseph's expression and the unspoken thoughts behind it. Joseph's barely discernible nod confirmed Nicodemus's guess was correct.

Turning to the one who had asked the question—a leading council member named Liam, a Levite who could be depended upon to expose and destroy heresies while paying false homage to Rome and fattening his own purse—Nicodemus gave his reluctant assent.

"Good," Liam replied. "We can use your levelheadedness. We must ascertain from this so-called prophet exactly who he is and report back to our Jerusalem brethren. There are far too many rumors about him. Some, as you all know, are more heretical than others. We are the declared guardians of Judaism—we must take this charge seriously." Liam's statement was greeted with nodding heads and murmurs of agreement. Liam then turned to the rest of the group and motioned that they should be on their way.

"We will meet back here in precisely one hour," Liam

instructed. "If we push the beasts, we can be there by midday," he added. In spite of his short stature and soft hands, Liam could command with a word and a raised eyebrow.

The room emptied quickly as each made his way to his home to make preparation for the journey to Bethany beyond Jordan, where they knew John the Baptizer met frequently with his followers.

***

Two hours later, still early in the morning, found them well on their way. Nicodemus thought they were making good time.

Joseph and Nicodemus had purposely allowed their camels to slow down, drifting to the back of the contingent of Pharisees, priests, and Sanhedrin members, with a few temple assistants, hangers-on, and wishful thinkers wanting to ingratiate themselves with the rulers. Nicodemus counted over thirty travelers—some carried weapons—a much larger number than had been in the temple meeting earlier. Some Nicodemus didn't know, and he wondered how they'd attached themselves to this mission. *Liam's doing, no doubt!*

Joseph asked loudly, clearly wanting to be overheard, "Nicodemus, my friend! We haven't been able to visit recently—how is your family? I heard of your wife's illness. I trust she is better."

Nicodemus, knowing the importance of hiding their true motivation for accompanying this assemblage, replied in kind. "Miriam is much better, my friend, owing to the prayers and ministrations of our faithful priests." He was gratified to notice the few eavesdroppers closest to them turn back to their conversations with their own companions.

Joseph, glancing ahead to make sure no one heard, replied softly, "How much did you have to pay?"

Nicodemus waved him to silence. Leaning closer to Joseph's camel, he whispered, "Too much, my friend, too much."

As the two followed behind the rest of the religious leaders, Nicodemus thought about the task before them. John the

Baptizer was preaching in the wilderness a message of repentance. To Nicodemus's ears, the message had a ring of truth—studied for centuries in the Torah—but unwelcome truth to the Sanhedrin and other leaders. *If John is who I suspect he is, then four hundred years of God's silence has been broken.*

Nicodemus thought it was safe for him and Joseph to speak their minds to each other now, so he asked Joseph the question burning in his mind.

"Joseph," he began softly, "what think you? Is this preacher Elijah come back from the dead to call us to repentance?"

"I think it's likely, my friend. Both Isaiah and Malachi agree in their description of the prophet who is to come. I believe the Baptizer is he, Elijah reincarnated."

Nicodemus pursed his lips as he considered Joseph's words.

"Perhaps he is not Elijah returned from the grave, but a new herald who echoes Elijah's words. Some of our teachers have said thus about those passages—that there are other interpretations."

Nicodemus lowered his voice even further. "Some have even said he might be the Christ."

Joseph pondered for a moment.

"My friend, I guess that's what we seek today—answers from this prophet."

Four hours later, having crossed the Jordan River, they now approached the area where John was known to preach and baptize. They could see him in the distance, hands raised in the center of a throng of seekers. His impassioned voice carried over the desert, strong and commanding, mingled with the sound of crying emanating from the people who crowded around him.

"This is the one I was talking about when I said, 'Someone is coming after me who is far greater than I am, for he existed long before me.'"

The rulers heard his words clearly. They stopped their camels a good distance away and dismounted on the top of a small hill overlooking the scene. A few people in the crowd turned and looked at them briefly, but their attention was all for the man they called a prophet, standing in their midst.

Leaving their camels in the care of their servants, the religious leaders descended the hill and were now at the edge of the circle. As John's words rang out, the rulers looked at each other, as if waiting for another to speak. Finally Liam began the interrogation for which they'd come.

"Who are you?" he called out over the crowd in a challenging tone.

John's answer cut right to the real question and didn't mince words.

"I am not the Messiah," John stated flatly, his gaze burning into Liam's.

Nicodemus was impressed with his boldness and plain language. John stood, hands on his hips—a giant of a man hardened by life in the desert, wearing his trademark camel's hair—and calmly stared Liam down. Nicodemus was sure this strange prophet could hold his own in a physical fight, even opposing several at a time. *He doesn't look as if he's concerned in the least.*

John's blunt reply seemed to stall the rulers for a moment. They looked to Liam. Nicodemus could see the bulge of veins at the back of Liam's neck, his irritation clearly getting the best of him.

"Well then, who are you?" Liam asked, none too politely.

John didn't reply. His followers were getting restive.

"I said, who are you then? Are you Elijah?" Liam said as he stepped through the throng slowly, the other rulers following. The crowd parted reluctantly to let them through, accompanied by dark looks and disgruntled murmurings.

Nicodemus looked warily around him. *This could get ugly!* He saw one of John's followers block Joseph's way with a hand to Joseph's chest. Joseph gently removed the man's hand and kept going. Joseph glanced at Nicodemus, shaking his head. Clearly, he had the same thought as Nicodemus—that it wouldn't take much to ignite this crowd into a violent mob to protect their so-called prophet.

The rulers were now standing directly in front of John, Liam the closest. The disparity in stature between them caused Liam to have to look up, even from a few feet away. As the rulers gathered into a tight little circle, John continued to stare, silently challenging them. His restless followers quieted until all that could be heard was the light breeze blowing over the dry hillside and the whimper of a baby somewhere in the crowd.

"No," John said, finally answering Liam's question, again with no other explanation.

Liam looked around at the other religious leaders, giving a slight nod to Nicodemus. He knew what Liam was asking of him. Liam didn't want to be the only voice challenging John—better it was a group effort than just one.

Nicodemus stepped forward and politely queried, "Are you the prophet we are expecting?"

"No."

Liam stepped closer to John. The veins in his neck seemed at the bursting point as he shook his fist in the prophet's face.

The midget confronting the giant, Nicodemus thought.

"Then who are you?" Liam shouted. "We need an answer for those who sent us! What have you to say for yourself?"

Nicodemus, standing next to Liam, laid a calming hand on his shoulder. Liam shook it off.

"Answer me! Who are you?"

John, looking out over the multitude, said loudly, "I am a voice shouting in the wilderness, 'Clear the way for the Lord's coming!'" His voice echoed over the hillside, and then silence descended once again.

Joseph leaned closer to Nicodemus and whispered, "We were right, my friend. Do you see it?"

Nicodemus, watching Liam closely, nodded his agreement.

Liam brazenly challenged John again. "If you aren't the Messiah or Elijah or the Prophet, what right do you have to baptize?"

Nicodemus was amazed at the man's audacity, given they were outnumbered three to one by this crowd.

The directness of Liam's accusation stirred the crowd again. Nicodemus felt the tension mount. He caught Liam's eye and shook his head.

Leaning over, he whispered, "No good will come of this confrontation, my friend."

Liam sniffed haughtily and looked away, ignoring his warning. Nicodemus felt Joseph's hand on his arm pulling him away from Liam, but he stood his ground.

"We must leave, my friend," came the whisper from Joseph, close to his ear. "Nothing good will be accomplished here."

"Yes, I agree, Joseph," Nicodemus whispered back. "But we mustn't leave ahead of Liam, nor leave him to this rabble."

Joseph reluctantly agreed.

Finally, John's answer to Liam's question lifted over the rulers and quieted the crowd once again.

"I baptize with water, but right here in the crowd is someone you do not recognize."

The rulers looked this way and that, trying to spot who John might be talking about.

John continued. "Though his ministry follows mine, I'm not even worthy to be his slave and untie the straps of his sandal."

Joseph grabbed Nicodemus's arm and whispered excitedly, "Nicodemus! Who else could he be talking about? 'Not even worthy to be his slave'? Who could it be but Messiah?"

Nicodemus frantically waved him to silence as he saw some in the crowd turn in their direction. He took a backward step away from Liam, tugging on Joseph's cloak. They walked a few feet away.

"You're rash, my friend! We must be careful—the council cares not to hear of Messiah. You know that!"

"Yes, yes, you're right. But what do you think? Is Messiah here, in this crowd?" Joseph's head turned quickly as he scanned the people around them.

Nicodemus shook his head. He noted the religious leaders

were now preparing to leave. It seemed, thankfully, that the confrontation was over. He hadn't heard Liam's response to John's statement, but now Liam was giving his parting shot at the strange prophet.

"Worthy or not," Liam said with a sneer, standing toe to toe with John, "we will be watching you. Do not think any of your heresies will escape our notice."

John, his feet planted in a wide stance, leaned forward slightly, bringing his face to within inches of Liam's. His answer took Nicodemus's breath away.

John threw his head back and laughed. He laughed! Nicodemus doubted if Liam had ever experienced such mocking behavior—certainly it was contrary to the fawning courtesy to which he was accustomed. Liam's face, clearly shocked, was suffused in purple.

"Priest, I will be happy to talk to you again. Do not think *you* have escaped the notice of the Lord. *He* watches both of us," John said boldly.

Clearly shaken, Liam gave a loud "Humph!" and turned—the leaders turning with him like a school of fish—and made his way back through the crowd. Complete silence followed them. John's followers glared at the religious leaders as they retreated. As they came to the top of the small hill, the leaders could hear John begin his preaching again. Liam stopped for a moment and turned back toward the Baptizer.

"Repent! For the kingdom of heaven is near..."

Liam shook his head angrily and mounted his camel, the entire company following suit. As they went down the back side of the hill, John's voice faded away.

It's difficult for us, living in the twenty-first century, to walk in Nicodemus's sandals. Living on this side of the cross, we take a lot for granted. We know how Jesus lived and how He died.

We have access to the messianic prophecies and can connect them almost effortlessly to their fulfillment. Nicodemus had no such privilege—where we look backward to the cross and immediately see Jesus as Messiah, Nicodemus looked forward into the unknown, seeking his Messiah.

He had been schooled in the Torah and the Law of Moses since a small boy; he knew the prophecies. His life had been steeped in the customs and practices of strict Judaism. He had trained as a lawyer and was now a member of the Jewish elite—the Sanhedrin.

As the Jewish court of law, the Sanhedrin was the last stop on the truth train for the Jewish people. They were the ultimate lawgivers and law adjudicators. Our Supreme Court is comparative, but only to a point. The Sanhedrin in the first century held ultimate authority over civil *and* spiritual law for the Jewish people.

With his rich heritage, training, and superior position, Nicodemus, along with Joseph of Arimathea, walked a fine line with their co-rulers. Coming to belief in Jesus of Nazareth as the long-awaited Messiah was tantamount to committing treason against Judaism—and the punishment would be severe.

Nicodemus and Joseph had much to consider as they traveled.

The religious leaders traveled in silence for the first half mile as they journeyed back to Jerusalem, roughly sixty miles southwest from Bethany beyond Jordan. Nicodemus noted their somber expressions, revealing how seriously they considered John's message. *We're in for some interesting times.*

He was proved right when Liam abruptly brought his camel to a halt. He turned around and put up his hand, signaling his followers to stop. Bringing his camel to its knees, he climbed to the ground, the other members of the council following his lead. They gathered around him.

"We're not going back yet," he announced bluntly, mouth in a tight line.

"What?" The question echoed around the group, puzzled expressions on every face. Liam held up his hand to quell the murmuring.

"This John the Baptizer is a dangerous man with a dangerous message. Can't you see it?" Liam demanded, looking at them in turn.

They eyed each other warily, clearly not following Liam's thought. Nicodemus and Joseph, however, exchanged knowing looks.

"What do you mean, Liam? He's just a crazy preacher, always making wild statements and stirring up trouble. The only people who listen to him are either just as crazy as he is, or they're mentally…you know…wanting. Why do you call him 'dangerous'?" Avner asked.

Liam regarded him with distaste. It was well known among the rulers that Liam, though cousin and guardian of the younger man, held no respect for him. Avner had no ambition and rarely understood the finer points of Judaism and its capacity to control the masses. Liam often said he wondered if he'd made a mistake allowing Avner to be a part of his inner circle. He'd once told Nicodemus he suspected Avner's mental prowess to be on a par with the mentally "deficient" of which he had just spoken.

"John the Baptizer is a fraud," he said brusquely. "He's another power-hungry, so-called prophet trying to bilk the poor people. But he's more than that. He could conceivably rouse enough people to his side to cause a rebellion against the Sanhedrin and Rome itself. He promises forgiveness of sins. That's blasphemy, as you well know! Only God can forgive sins—not this dreamer."

He broke off to let his words sink in. "We must stay and see what else he's up to. Agreed?"

They looked at each other reluctantly. Nicodemus read their expressions—clearly they struggled with fear of the consequences if they refused obedience to Liam.

We all know what Liam's capable of and that he operates with impunity.

"Good," Liam said, not hearing any objections. "Now we must find places to stay. And I'll send a messenger back to Jerusalem with our plan."

That settled, they climbed back onto their camels and changed direction for the small village nearby to find accommodations.

***

The next day, they traveled again to where John was preaching—a somewhat smaller group this time, having left their camels behind. As they walked, Nicodemus and Joseph talked privately, taking care to keep their voices low and casual.

"Did you sleep well, Nicodemus?"

"Hardly at all, my friend. I couldn't get the preacher's words out of my head. I think we're headed for some trouble. Our friends on the council have no idea who they're dealing with—not that I do—but them even less so."

"I agree," Joseph answered. "I couldn't sleep much either." He moved closer to Nicodemus. "I'm beginning to believe that John is Messiah's herald and that Messiah is here…or almost here."

"Be careful, Joseph. We know there have been many false messiahs and there will be many more." He hesitated, carefully scanning the men around them. None even glanced in their direction.

"But," he added, leaning closer to Joseph, "I too am leaning that way in my thoughts."

They walked in silence then, Nicodemus praying for wisdom and clarity of thought.

They found John standing on the bank of the Jordan River amid an even larger throng of seekers. Nicodemus thought his hair was even wilder and more unkempt looking than yesterday, his camel-hair tunic belted tightly around the waist, muscles and sinews straining in fervent passion. As they came nearer, Nicodemus could see he was dripping wet, as were a few of the people around him. Many of them were on their knees before him, some weeping.

"...I am a voice shouting in the wilderness, 'Prepare the way for the Lord's coming! Clear the road for him!'"

Liam snorted in anger. "More of the same, my friends," he said loudly.

The Baptizer looked straight at Liam then, his fanatical eyes boring into Liam's, his face ablaze.

"You brood of snakes!" he shouted. "Who warned you to flee God's coming wrath? Prove by the way you live that you have repented of your sins and turned to God."

Liam reacted to that with two fists raised in the air.

"How dare you speak to us like this! We are your rulers—you must obey us or face the consequences, sinner!"

The crowd parted to let Liam through, Nicodemus and Joseph right behind him. The rest of the rulers hung back.

It was as if John hadn't heard Liam's words.

"Don't just say to each other, 'We're safe, for we are descendants of Abraham,'" John said pointedly. "That means nothing, for I tell you, God can create children of Abraham from these very stones—"

"Means nothing?" Liam interrupted John's admonitions. His voice rang out over the throng. He turned away from John then and faced the people.

"You heard him—he speaks lies! Saying we mean nothing, that we are the descendants of Father Abraham...and it means nothing!"

The crowd stirred restlessly. Nicodemus could see Liam's words swayed a few, but many looked confused.

Clearly Liam was reading the crowd the same way. He turned to face John again.

"Well? What have you to say for yourself, Baptizer? We

await your pleasure," Liam said with a sneer.

The breeze was the only answer. Nicodemus judged a full minute had gone by. During that minute, John and Liam stared each other down. Neither would budge. John glared at the religious rulers, then lifted his eyes to the crowd and answered, stoking Liam's fiery rage.

"Even now the ax of God's judgment is poised, ready to sever the roots of the trees. Yes, every tree that does not produce good fruit will be chopped down and thrown into the fire."

Silence fell over the throng again. Then Nicodemus heard the fear-filled murmurings around him.

"What are we to do?"

"How can we save ourselves?"

"What does he mean, 'good fruit'?"

Liam answered them. "You can save yourselves by not listening to this *traitor*!"

A collective gasp at the word *traitor*.

Liam continued, his voice firm with passionate conviction. "Yes, *traitor*! He speaks against your rulers and against Rome itself! He comes to destroy our most sacred religion."

Liam was now standing next to John, arms open as if to gather the people to himself.

"Listen, my beloved people," his voice, softer now, dripped with compassion. His restless listeners quieted.

"Listen to me," Liam went on. "There are many false prophets in the land. This man"—he waved his hand in John's direction—"is but one more. You know the way to be absolved of your sin, and it is not here. Go to the temple, offer the correct sacrifices, allow your priests to cleanse your sins. Do not be swayed by every wind of teaching." His words were measured, reasoned, calm.

Even Nicodemus's heart was somehow soothed by Liam's softly spoken words. He gently led them into familiar territory and reminded them of what they'd been taught for centuries. John's words brought unsettled confusion. Liam's words lit the path they'd followed since God had spoken to Father Abraham on the mountain.

But a warning inner voice reminded Nicodemus of Liam's true character. *He's as greedy and grasping as any of the rulers. And he hates the people. Surely they can see through this!*

Joseph leaned in to whisper to Nicodemus.

"Nicodemus, say something! These poor people need to know who he is and that..."

But John wasn't finished yet. His powerful voice rushed at them, destroying their peace once again.

"I baptize with water those who repent of their sins and turn to God. But someone is coming soon who is greater than I am—so much greater that I'm not worthy even to be his slave and carry his sandals. He will baptize you with the Holy Spirit and with fire."

Liam roared, head shaking in unrestrained fury, spittle flying. "Holy Spirit? What 'Holy Spirit' is that, false prophet? You speak blasphemy!"

Joseph moved in again, hissing in Nicodemus's ear.

"My friend, we must put an end to this. It can't possibly end well. We must retreat and leave John to his preaching. Liam's out of control—he doesn't know the danger he's in."

Nicodemus nodded, gripping Joseph's arm. But as he moved to take Liam's arm, John spoke again.

"He is ready to separate the chaff from the wheat with his winnowing fork," John said, voice quieter, but no less passionate. "Antipas is one such as these. He calls himself Herod, ruler of Galilee, yet he takes his brother's wife. Judgment awaits him!"

John's eyes bored into Liam's. The crowd had stilled to hear the prophet's words.

"Then, priest, he will clean up the threshing area, gathering the wheat into his barn but burning the chaff with never-ending fire."

Nicodemus heard the threat in those words—and clearly Liam understood also. Nicodemus had never seen him like this. He moved closer to hold him back should he launch himself at

John. But Liam only glared at the Baptizer, jaw and arm muscles clenched, fists doubled up at his sides. Abruptly he turned and, waving the other rulers to follow, walked quickly through the throng as they opened a path before him.

Once again Joseph fell into step next to Nicodemus. They said nothing, which suited Nicodemus just fine, as he turned over in his mind what they'd just seen and heard.

One of the younger rulers, walking in the back of the group, called out to Liam.

"Sir, don't we have enough to take him now?"

Liam stopped, turned, and replied quietly, his fury evidently tempered for the moment. "That is not our purpose. We are here to observe and report. We must prove his claims false."

The other replied, "But you goaded him, sir, into revealing his blasphemous teachings. Surely we have enough! Why wait?"

The eagerness of the younger man to take immediate action resonated in several others, evidenced by the nodding heads. But Nicodemus knew Liam for a careful man—he was sure he would not be so rash as to take matters into his own hands yet. He was proved right when Liam spoke.

"Enough! I regret my show of temper. But, as you say, it did serve to reveal to us what this charlatan is about. He threatens us—the leaders of Judaism, the keepers of the faith! This will not do…it simply won't do. He attempts to mount an insurrection by accusing Herod Antipas of a crime! He's rash, my friends—and his rashness will be his undoing. Nay, we will continue to observe, to ask questions. Our Jerusalem brothers have given us this task, and we will complete it. No more talk of arresting him—yet. Do you understand?" Liam waited for a response.

Nicodemus finally spoke up. "Yes, I agree with you Liam—no action yet. We'll all keep our ears to the ground."

"Thank you, Nicodemus. I knew I could count on you to back me up. Now, let's get back to the village and continue our investigations. Perhaps we should split up and mingle in the streets and the market, get the peasants talking and discover what they know. But we must be discreet and not give away our real purpose." With those words, Liam turned and continued on toward the town.

Nicodemus breathed easier. His purpose was different from Liam's. He was glad he would have more time to discover the truth—but not the truth Liam was seeking.

John the Baptist was not afraid to speak against the religious rulers of his day. He spoke the uncompromising truth to his followers and his enemies with no apology, no equivocation, no compromise. He lost his head over it. Herod was incensed at John's criticism of his marital affairs. Herod was also afraid of John's popularity with the common people, and so he rid himself of the problem by imprisoning him and later beheading him.

Truth takes a beating in today's world, just as it did in John's.

Is God the Creator of all life everywhere?

Does life begin at conception?

Did God create gender?

Did God make the blueprint for marriage?

Did God know yesterday that I would be single today? Does He see? Does He care?

Is there truly only one way to reach heaven?

Does He always keep His promises?

The simple answer to these foundational questions—answered in the Scriptures for us—is a resounding *Yes!*

But we, in our finite wisdom, wrestle with infinite God over these questions, redefining life on planet earth to suit ourselves. We think we are so smart, so innovative, so progressive—but we forget that cultures throughout history have participated in the same wrestling match, beginning with the serpent's question to Eve: "Did God say..."

Each time I've asked "Did God say…" and have answered from my own pitiful store of "truth," it has led me away from my Redeemer and into heartache.

Did God say…He has a unique plan for my life? One that would bring glory to Him and peace to my heart?

Did God say…I should await His timing for that plan?

Did God say…I will be your light, even as you walk in the darkest places of life?

Did God say…do not fear for yourself or your family, for I am working where you cannot see?

Did God say…I will come and take you to the place I've prepared for you?

And more.

I've listened to God's adversary too many times—as did Eve—and bit the fruit that killed relationship with my Redeemer, closed my eyes to His all-surpassing grace, and led me down the rocky path of disobedience and chaos.

But God is patient. He has always drawn me back, made me look into the mirror and behold what I've done—hurt myself, hurt my family, and brought dishonor to the Name above every name. I can't go back. I can't retrace my steps and start over. I can't erase the hurt I've caused.

Did God say…if you confess your sin, I am faithful and just and will forgive your sin and cleanse you from all unrighteousness? *Yes, He did!*

Truth is unpalatable sometimes, is it not? It's hard to speak it, and it's hard to hear sometimes. But we must not shrink from it—both from the hearing of it and the telling of it.

Truth about ourselves will cleanse our hearts—if we choose to heed it. Truth given to others may lead them to salvation, peace, and a life of service to God. We must choose truth in every instance. Our mothers and fathers were right. *Tell the truth, even when it hurts!*

Dear brothers and sisters, let's be like John in our day, shall we?

Nicodemus and Joseph had planned to meet privately for the evening meal. As they sat together at a small booth in the marketplace, Nicodemus brooded over the day's events. They'd both wandered the streets, casually speaking to people they met. They had seen others of their company doing the same, blending in and gathering information as Liam had instructed.

There's so much to sort out. I've never been a spy before and I don't like it – I much prefer the head-on approach to issues.

Nicodemus wondered how it would all end.

As he broke off a piece of bread and dipped it in oil, he glanced at Joseph and guessed his thoughts ran the same course as his own. *Is Messiah here?*

"My friend, your thoughts. Where do they lead you?" Nicodemus finally asked.

"I spoke to an old woman today. She told me she believes the Baptizer is Elijah's ghost, heralding the coming judgment. I spoke to two shepherds who think Messiah is here now. And still another believes John is Messiah. And several others think he's a snake-oil salesman, promising fairy-tale endings for a price." Joseph looked at Nicodemus. "I don't know what to think. My thoughts lead me around in circles!"

"I had the same experience. People I spoke to said similar things. It seems no two people believe the same about John. But, Joseph, I then spoke to two children, who state categorically—probably parroting their parents—Messiah is here and John is his prophet, telling everyone to get ready for his public appearance," Nicodemus said.

Joseph thought for a moment and then looked up at his friend. "Well," he said with new conviction, "those two children may have hit the mark, don't you think? Their words are the nearest to what the prophets have foretold about Messiah. Could it be?"

Nicodemus, his lawyer's mind laying out each fact about Messiah—written long ago by the prophets—in logical order like bricks on a road, slowly nodded.

"Yes, you could be right," he said softly, eyes locked on Joseph's for a long moment.

Nicodemus started violently when Liam clapped him on the shoulder.

"So at last I find you!" Liam said jovially, plopping down next to him.

How long has he been there? What did he overhear?

Nicodemus tried to be casual as he returned Liam's greeting. Joseph watched warily, white faced.

"Liam! Have you eaten? Would you like to join us? It looks like there'd still be enough for you." Nicodemus handed him a piece of bread, but Liam waved it away.

"No, no, go ahead and finish your meal," he answered generously. Nicodemus and Joseph visibly relaxed.

Then Liam leaned in a little closer and grabbed Joseph firmly by the arm. Joseph froze.

"My friends," Liam said in a conspiratorial whisper, "of what do you speak so quietly? I've been watching you from over there." He pointed to the pottery stall only a few feet away. "You looked as if you have secrets to keep."

Neither answered him.

"Come…come—you can tell me," he urged, his face giving nothing away.

Nicodemus said, trying not to appear nervous, "Well, we talked to—"

He didn't get to finish. Liam excitedly broke in, letting go of Joseph's arm.

"Yes, yes, you talked to many people, as did I. And I'll warrant you dug up as much dirt on this crazy preacher and his so-called 'coming' messiah as I did. Am I right?" Liam asked eagerly.

Inwardly, Nicodemus sighed in relief.

"Yes, of course, Liam. We talked to many people who are just plain confused about the Baptizer's message. But," Nicodemus said honestly, "there are many people who believe him."

Liam sniffed in disgust. "Yes, I heard from some of those. And it will only serve to get the Baptizer what he deserves—his head separated from his body. And I guarantee you, when certain words are repeated to Antipas, *that* will be a foregone conclusion. He's swaying the poor peasants into heresy. This is exactly the kind of report we must take back to Jerusalem."

Nicodemus gave a sidelong glance at Joseph.

"Yes, I guess so, Liam."

"'Guess so'? You don't sound very convincing, Nicodemus."

Nicodemus, smoothing over Liam's challenge, said, "I just meant that we must be very sure of our facts, very clear, so we can make an irrefutable case in Jerusalem. That's all."

"Ah, yes, that's exactly it, Nicodemus," Liam answered excitedly, clearly taken in by Nicodemus's assertion. "You and I have the same mind, and it relieves me mightily. I know how completely honest you are, and your word will carry much weight in Jerusalem."

Nicodemus breathed a little easier as Liam went on.

"I've talked to most of the others, and they agree. I think we need stay only one more day, and then we can head back to Jerusalem. Good news, right?" Liam rubbed his hands together.

Nicodemus was unimpressed. *He thinks he's done us a favor.*

Joseph, finally finding his voice, replied, "Uh, yes, good news, Liam."

Liam stood and glanced around the market, a look of disgust on his face.

"Well, I'm going back to that hovel they call an inn. The dust and the smell of these commoners are simply too much for me. Early start tomorrow, my friends!" With that pronouncement, Liam left them.

"That was close," Joseph said to Nicodemus. "Do you think he heard what we said?"

"No, probably not. He was fishing—and, as always, I think he was too full of himself to pay attention to us," Nicodemus replied. "Come on, Joseph. Let's go back to our tents. Like Liam, I want to get plenty of sleep tonight. I want a clear head tomorrow."

"Yes, and I'd much rather be in my own tent tonight than in that 'hovel,' as Liam calls it. I've heard stories of much carousing there. I'm surprised Liam would stay there."

Nicodemus, with a wry grin, said, "I'm not. You don't know him like I do."

With that they turned and made their way from the market to where they'd pitched their tents just outside of town.

The position in which Nicodemus and Joseph find themselves might resonate with you, as it does me. They had religious freedom—but only *if* they mind-melded with the rules of Judaism and *if* they adhered to each command added to the Law of Moses by the priests.

We have religious freedom—*if* we don't talk about our faith in our workplaces, our schools, our government, and in our military. Our politically correct rules, put into place while we played with our screens and toys, have done their work—transformed the army of believers who march on their knees into a cloistered, silent mass, afraid of their own shadows.

It's time we wake up and realize this: if we don't fearlessly talk about the loving God who saves us and keeps us, disdaining the consequences, there will be no next generation of believers, and that will be on us.

Nicodemus and Joseph stand on the precipice of belief that Jesus is Messiah. We already believe—and we must not keep silent, even if it means we lose our jobs, our freedom, or our lives. The martyred who have gone before now bask in the perfect presence and goodness of God, and they shout to this generation that persecution and death for the Name of Jesus is nothing compared to the eternal weight of glory they now enjoy.

And because of *their* valiant, relentless witness, we have been brought to the sharp point of decision: follow Christ into eternity, or follow Satan into eternity.

Early the next afternoon found Liam and his entourage heading south to Jerusalem. They moved slowly in the hot afternoon sun, not wishing to push their camels too hard. Quiet conversations could be heard as these keepers of Judaism discussed all they'd seen and heard.

After spending the early morning mingling with townspeople, they had again made their way to the Jordan, where John still ministered. However, by the time they'd arrived at the river, John was finished for the day. They could see him moving through the throng, counseling and praying with individuals. Then he quietly moved away, walking slowly into the wilderness, alone. Soon he arrived at the top of a small hill, turned and looked back, then disappeared down the other side. Liam watched him intently until he was gone.

Nicodemus, standing near Liam, heard him say softly, "We'll meet again, my friend. Depend upon it." He broke off abruptly, moving away when he noticed Nicodemus watching him.

Many of the seekers stood in small groups, chattering about what had just happened there—what the rulers had just missed.

Nicodemus and Joseph paid careful attention to the excited babble all around them. Several threw suspicious glances their way, but the people were so full of what they'd just witnessed that they couldn't contain themselves, even in the presence of their religious rulers.

Their attention turned to an elderly man, bent over, clothes dripping wet. His few wisps of straggly hair were plastered to his head and face; the skin on his thin arms hung loosely; his ragged robes all but fell off his body. But the joy glowing from his face made his dreary poverty seem incidental, almost inconsequential—the man's countenance exuded a richness, a satisfaction, a peace that belied his earthly state.

"He's come! He's come!" the old man declared delightedly to the people around him. "I've been baptized, and my sins are forgiven. The herald of the Most High declared it to me!"

The little man's ancient singsong voice was captivating, and soon he had the whole crowd clapping and dancing along with him. Nicodemus thought it was the most beautiful thing he'd seen in his whole life.

In the next moment, the joy of the throng was crushed.

Liam grabbed the old man by the arm and demanded an explanation. Squinting against the bright sunlight, the startled man shrank back from the priest. Liam, short of stature as he was, towered over the man.

"Speak, old man! What about this so-called baptism?" Liam shouted harshly, sweat dripping on his brow.

His priestly turban slipped sideways, and he reached up to right it, causing it to slip the other way and fall to the ground. Avner hurried forward and picked it up. He tried to hand it to Liam, who rudely pushed him away, causing him to drop it in the dirt again. As it fell, the linen partially unwound. Once again, Avner picked it up, trying to put it back together.

"Leave off!" Liam roared, throwing a fist in his cousin's direction. Avner backed away, still holding the turban.

Once more, Liam, now looking smaller without his priestly headdress, turned his attention to the man he still held like a vise.

The old man, face creased in fear, stayed silent under Liam's red-faced glare. Liam roughly shook the old man, ripping a larger hole in the man's tattered sleeve. Wincing in pain, the man tried to escape Liam's grasp, but the priest's iron grip was unbreakable. The heat and the tension were unbearable as the agitated throng closed around them. Angry whispers circled on the wind.

Nicodemus pushed through the crowd, apprehensive as Liam continued abusing the old man. Just as he arrived at Liam's side, a younger man stepped forward.

"Please, grandfather, answer the priest," he pleaded.

Haltingly, in a frightened voice, the old man recounted the story.

"I repented, and the prophet baptized me. Then…then…a man came to the river. He walked right up to the prophet and asked to be baptized with the rest of us."

"What man?" Liam interrupted, shaking him again.

The old man didn't answer Liam's question. Clearly gathering his courage, the old man continued as if Liam hadn't interrupted him. Nothing could stop him now—the words flowed as fast as the Jordan River at high flood stage.

"But John said, 'I am the one who needs to be baptized by you, so why are you coming to me?' The man Jesus answered the prophet and said, 'It should be done, for we must carry out all that God requires.' And so the prophet baptized Jesus. That's all, sir. I swear, that's all," the old man finished.

Liam let go of him, pushing him away so hard that he fell to the ground. The priest turned away with a look of disgust. The younger man hurried to his grandfather's side and helped him up, and then they turned and disappeared into the sea of people.

Avner said wonderingly, looking after them, "Could it be true?"

Liam dismissed the tale with a wave of his hand.

"Utter nonsense," he said, then more loudly, "Complete, utter nonsense!"

Nicodemus wasn't so sure. *Liam wears religious blinders – he does not understand the significance of the old man's witness.*

His secret judgment was borne out when another in the crowd called out, "Remember what happened? As Jesus approached John to be baptized, while still some ways off, John cried out, 'Look! The Lamb of God who takes away the sin of the world! He is the one I was talking about when I said, "A man is coming after me who is far greater than I am, for he existed long before me." I did not recognize him as Messiah, but I have been baptizing with water so that he might be revealed to Israel.'"

And still another.

"I saw Jesus came up out of the water, and his face was ablaze with joy as he looked heavenward. Did you see him? He seemed to hear something we couldn't. And then the dove—remember? The dove came down from heaven and sat on his shoulder!"

All around them, heads nodded and faces shone with wonder.

Nicodemus watched Liam's face as the witnesses exuberantly shared what they'd seen. The priest's eyes were narrowed, calculating. Clearly Liam thought this was what they'd come to discover. The witness's next words clinched it.

"And John said, 'I saw the Holy Spirit descending like a dove from heaven and resting upon him. I didn't know he was the one, but when God sent me to baptize with water, he told me, "The one on whom you see the Spirit descend and rest is the one who will baptize with the Holy Spirit." I saw this happen to Jesus, so I testify that he is the Chosen One of God.'"

Damning words, Nicodemus thought. *But likely the truth.*

Liam reacted in characteristic fashion by admonishing the throng of seekers to come to the temple and pay the required price for their forgiveness or suffer the consequences. Then he strode to Avner, jerked his turban away from him, dusted it off, and jammed it back on his head. He didn't get it on quite straight though, and the religious rulers retreated to the muted sounds of giggling. Liam's face looked set in stone as they remounted their camels.

During the long, hot journey back to Jerusalem, Nicodemus concocted his plan—a plan he would not even share with Joseph—a plan to meet Jesus and get his own answers.

***

Arriving in Jerusalem some hours later, Nicodemus went straight home. Too weary to even eat a delayed evening meal, he kissed his wife, Miriam, and went immediately to bed. His Pharisaical mind was in turmoil over all he'd seen take place at the Jordan River, all he'd heard from the witnesses, and all he knew to be true from Holy Writ about Messiah.

He recalled, as he tossed and turned, that as soon as they'd arrived back in Jerusalem, a messenger had arrived, hot and exhausted, and held a whispered conference with Liam. All Nicodemus had heard of the conversation as he'd turned his camel toward home were the phrases "wedding in Cana" and "miracle…he turned the water into wine!" Nicodemus was sure they were talking about Jesus of Nazareth—Liam's darkened expression gave it away.

Another tidbit of information came back to him now. As they were leaving the area of the Jordan River earlier in the day, they'd heard that two of John's followers had defected to Jesus. *What does that mean?*

And, further back in his memory, events from thirty years ago surfaced. He'd been a young man, barely out of his childhood, when his father had burst into their small home and shocked them with a tale he'd heard at the Jerusalem synagogue—the brutal slaying of all boys under the age of two in the region of Bethlehem, ordered by Herod, to silence the rampant rumors going about that Messiah was born. Nicodemus's father had played it down at the time, saying these rumors were being put about by poor, illiterate shepherds. But still, his father and mother were aghast at what Herod had done.

Nicodemus remembered asking his father what it meant.

"Father, why would Herod do that? They were babies! What could they have done to warrant such treatment?"

His father chose to divert his attention from the uncomfortable question.

"Nicodemus," his father had said, always using Nicodemus's questions as teaching moments, "the mothers of

Bethlehem are weeping for their lost boys. Tell me of a similar time you recall from your studies."

Nicodemus thought for a moment; then the verses came to him.

"The prophet Jeremiah, Father. He said, 'A cry is heard in Ramah—deep anguish and bitter weeping. Rachel weeps for her children, refusing to be comforted—for her children are gone.' Is that correct, Father?"

"Yes, my son. It seems that time is being repeated in ours," his father responded sadly with a pat on his son's head.

"But, Father," Nicodemus persisted, "what does it mean?"

His father had shaken his head and murmured, "I don't know, my son. I don't know. It's dangerous to ask too many questions."

The memory now slipped away in the night as Nicodemus rolled over and tried to sleep again. He felt a great foreboding. All his legal training in Judaism, all the teaching he'd endured as a child, and all his experience with the Sanhedrin were stacked up on one side of the balance scale in his mind. On the other side of the scale was one thing—Jesus of Nazareth—*Messiah? What is the truth?* Nicodemus thought he'd never sleep again until he had the answer.

***

Liam had given the council members one day at home with their families but expected them to resume their duties the next day. Two days after arriving back in Jerusalem, nearly Passover, Nicodemus arose early. His mind was still in turmoil, but he hid it from Miriam. He didn't want to worry her. And he certainly didn't want to put her in danger by sharing his plan to meet secretly with Jesus of Nazareth.

After inspecting their growing herds—neglected during his unexpected journey north—and seeing to one or two other chores Miriam had given him, they sat down to a simple breakfast of bread and fruit.

"Husband, I heard some disturbing rumors while you were

gone," Miriam said casually.

He reached and took her hand, so much smaller than his. She was a dainty woman but could be fierce if her emotions were roused. Her long dark hair and flashing brown eyes had captivated him from the moment he'd met her at the age of twenty. She'd been contracted at a very young age to another man, but he'd been killed, and no other contract had been pursued. It had taken quite a bit of convincing—months of discussion, in fact, between her parents and his—before consent was finally given for their marriage. Nicodemus always felt a little guilty about his feelings of gratitude at the other man's death.

"What rumors, my dear? Women's gossip at the market?" he gently asked.

"Well, I did hear it at the market the other day, from Anna and her cousin, Ariana, but what has that to do with it? You speak as if news heard at the market is always untrue. Or is it because I heard it from women?" Miriam asked pointedly.

"I'm sorry, wife. I didn't mean to...I meant..." He noticed the smile playing around Miriam's lips.

"You're teasing me, aren't you?"

"Yes, I am, Nicodemus. I missed you so while you were gone—I just couldn't resist."

They laughed together. Nicodemus wondered again what he'd ever do without her.

"What news did you hear?" he asked again, biting into a thick slice of Miriam's bread, baked just yesterday.

"We heard there was some disturbance, something about a confrontation between the prophet John and that odious priest Liam. They say Liam was shouting, challenging John, calling him a heretic. Is it true?"

"Well, you know Liam—he never backs away from a fight, even if it makes no sense. And I'd be very careful about the names you choose to call him," Nicodemus replied. He squeezed her shoulder, leaning over to plant a kiss on her forehead.

Miriam made a face at him.

"Don't be concerned about it, Miriam. No one was hurt. John left the area and went to wherever he makes his home—in the desert somewhere. We'll probably never have to deal with him again." He didn't believe that, but he didn't want Miriam to worry.

"Anna said he was making wild claims about Messiah. Is that true?" She picked a grape out of the basket of fruit between them.

Nicodemus couldn't risk her knowing what was in his mind, so he downplayed his answer as much as he could.

"He's always making wild claims. That's what these dreamers always do, sweetheart. We must try to sift through what they say and discern what's true and what's false. And that's just what I and the rest of the council will do today."

Nicodemus arose from the table.

"And now I must be going. I can't be late for this meeting. I'll see you for dinner, my dear."

He told her goodbye, kissed her again, and made his way to the temple, where he would meet with the council. Nicodemus dreaded it. He didn't know how long he'd be able to hide his misgivings about Liam's mission to destroy the Baptizer or his own growing conviction about Jesus of Nazareth.

***

The first face he saw as he approached the temple courtyard was Joseph, who hurried to him, a look of consternation on his face. Nicodemus heard shouting and thumping emanating from the inner courtyard.

"Nicodemus, you're finally here!" Joseph said, out of breath.

"My friend, why the agitation? What's happened? And what's all the commotion inside?"

"It's that Jesus of Nazareth, the one John baptized. He arrived in Jerusalem late last evening, according to reports. And now he's tearing up the temple, throwing out the sellers of sacrifices! I tell you—I've never seen anything like it. We must do something, Nicodemus!"

Nicodemus and Joseph hurried into the Court of the Gentiles, where sacrifices were sold to people too poor to bring their own or who had traveled too far to keep them alive. The moneychangers were also engaged, sitting at their makeshift tables, changing foreign currencies into acceptable forms for the temple tax—currency sometimes depicting gods and goddesses that were considered an abomination to the Jews.

As Nicodemus entered the courtyard, his first sight of Jesus of Nazareth was breathtaking. No longer the mild man described by John's followers during the previous days, Jesus was upending a heavy table, scattering coins, and breaking lamps. The noise—of the table crashing to its side and taking the lamp with it, the moneychanger screaming at Jesus, and the people yelling and trying to get out of Jesus's way—had never been seen or heard in the holy temple. Dust flew as Jesus moved from table to table, muscles bulging, picking up tables, chairs, and people and tossing them out of his way.

Jesus was beside himself—that much was obvious. But his movements were calm, deliberate, no hurry in his stride. He was angry, no doubt about it, but his anger was measured, calculating, as if he was not surprised by what he found and knew exactly what must be done.

And now Nicodemus could hear his words. He had one hapless moneychanger by the neck of his robe, hauling him toward the outer door, with a makeshift whip in the other hand, flicking it at the moneychanger's back as he strode toward the door.

"You're done here, thief! Get out and don't come back!" he declared in a firm voice, heaving the man out the door. Jesus then turned around and surveyed the scene, dust settling, as silence descended.

"You!" Jesus called out suddenly, pointing to the dove sellers. "Get these things out of here! Stop turning my Father's house into a marketplace!" They lost no time in packing up their tables and birds—some of which escaped and frantically flapped their wings in the vendors' faces—and running out.

Nicodemus thought it was the most refreshing scene he'd ever witnessed. *The usury charged by these merchants has always left a bad taste in my mouth, and worse, the religious leaders always look the other way while lining their own pockets.* If he could have, he'd have laughed out loud at the sight of the dove sellers as they scurried around the courtyard trying to recapture their birds, while at the same time trying to avoid being cornered and grabbed by Jesus.

He looked around for Joseph. Their eyes met, and Nicodemus knew they were both thinking the same thing, a prophecy regarding Messiah, penned by King David long ago.

Passion for God's house will consume me.

Once again studying the scene, Jesus began picking up hastily discarded account scrolls, ripping them to shreds. He cleaned up the pieces of broken lamps and shooed a stray dove out of the temple. Nicodemus, Joseph, and several other council members watched him in silence. Clearly, no one knew what to say.

The silence was broken by Liam, who'd come in quietly and had not made his presence known until now. As his voice rang out over the Court of the Gentiles, everyone turned to face him.

"What are you doing? If God gave you authority to do this, show us a miraculous sign to prove it."

Jesus stared at Liam for a few seconds, looking him up and down, eyes narrowed. Nicodemus, standing a few feet away, had a clear view of both men's faces.

It's as if Jesus of Nazareth knows Liam inside and out!

Then came the death-knell words, the words Nicodemus knew would be remembered and dragged out by the rulers when needed.

Jesus, in an almost offhand way as he righted another table, said quietly, "All right. Destroy this temple, and in three days I will raise it up."

Pandemonium broke out among the rulers. *"Blasphemy!"* echoed around the group, along with other choice words.

One voice, from an ambitious young ruler whom Nicodemus didn't know well, rose above the others.

"What?" he exclaimed. "What? It has taken forty-six years to build this temple, and you can rebuild it in three days?"

They waited for Jesus's answer, but it didn't come immediately. He turned his back on the rulers and strode leisurely toward the outer entrance. At the last moment he turned once again, and with an enigmatic grin splitting his face, he said, "My friends, be certain I can. You must, however, be clear on one thing. What temple am I talking about?" And with that astounding question hanging in the air, he made his way out and down the steps of the Royal Porch.

Joseph had moved quietly to Nicodemus's side. He started to say something, but Nicodemus cut him off.

"Not now, my friend," he whispered, waving a hand in the direction of the small knot of rulers who had followed Jesus to the entrance. "We must listen."

The rulers had started whispering among themselves but were getting louder in their anger and consternation at Jesus's parting shot.

"Liam, we could take him on the strength of what he's said here, in our presence, this day. Why do you hesitate?"

"I agree," Liam answered with a look at Nicodemus and Joseph. He waved them over. "My friends, what do you think?" he asked in a challenging tone.

Joseph looked at the floor, clearly not wanting to answer Liam.

Nicodemus said carefully, "That was surely enough to report to the rest of the court, Liam. It sounded to my ears like the very definition, legally, of blasphemy." Nicodemus paused. "But is it enough for Rome? Our masters there don't put much stock in our definition of blasphemy."

His question had the intended effect.

Liam didn't answer Nicodemus's question directly. Instead, he paced back and forth among them for a moment, hand cupping his chin in deep thought. The rest waited respectfully.

Joseph, standing next to Nicodemus, laid a hand on his arm, a question in his eyes. Nicodemus gave a barely discernible shake of his head.

"Yes, we do have enough—for ourselves—to charge him with blasphemy. He has told us this day that he considers *himself* to have authority over our most sacred temple, the dwelling place of God himself from ages past. He as much as said there is a temple other than the one God has given us. He will not get away with these treasonous statements, I can assure you." Liam paused.

"But, Nicodemus, my friend," he continued, "you are right. Rome doesn't think much of our cherished traditions and our duty to God. So we must continue to watch this pretender. The only crime we can successfully present to Rome is an assault on Rome herself. If we can find such a charge against him, then rest assured, Rome will bring her might down on his head. My friends, if you see or hear anything we can use—anything treasonous—you must immediately report to me. Agreed?"

Everyone nodded their heads and dispersed.

Nicodemus and Joseph waited until they were outside the courtyard and walking down the steps before speaking.

"What are you thinking, Nicodemus?" Joseph asked.

Nicodemus casually glanced around before speaking.

"I've been given a little more time, my friend. I'm more convinced than ever that I must speak to Jesus of Nazareth privately, before another sun rises," he replied, deciding to let Joseph in on his plan.

Joseph didn't look surprised and didn't miss a beat.

"What temple do *you* think Jesus was talking about?"

"I have an idea about that," Nicodemus answered thoughtfully. He looked at Joseph. "I think you do too—am I right?"

"Yes, you are. We Jews like to remember the prophets telling us Messiah will come to overthrow our Roman masters, setting up his kingdom of peace with us sitting next to him; but we conveniently forget the prophecies regarding his suffering. We don't even try to imagine what that means."

"Yes, Joseph, but I intend to find out, this night if I can."

"Be careful, Nicodemus. Make sure you're not followed," Joseph warned.

"Yes, I will. I will call on you tomorrow."

The two men had come to a junction in the street where they would part, each going to their homes. They stood for a moment, gazing out over the Passover crowd, jostling, calling out good-natured greetings to each other as they made their way to the temple or to the marketplace. Thoughts swirled in Nicodemus's head as he marked children, old people, and vendors going about their usual business.

They don't know that the world has shifted this day, by the words of one man. God help me if I'm wrong.

After a last look into Joseph's face, Nicodemus veered off toward home.

Have you allowed the words of Jesus to change your world? From Genesis to Revelation, God's Word speaks change to the world. But it means nothing if we, as individuals, do not allow it to change us.

My world changed when I was fourteen. I allowed the words of Jesus to change me. I clearly remember the day—June 23, 1968—when I decided, even at that tender age, that my path was headed in the wrong direction. God had allowed me to hear His Word in various instances over the course of the previous few months, and that date in the late sixties was the culmination. I believed, not even fully understanding what I was believing, and in a blink the path of my life was remade by the One Who made me. God took care of my lack of understanding—is still taking care of it—and set me on a course of walking in His footsteps.

I've messed up, left His company, made tragic choices, and

suffered tragic consequences, but God was always just around the bend, beckoning me back to Him. I haven't "arrived" yet—won't until He takes me home—but the path of belief and obedience continues, and I can truly say I wouldn't want to be anywhere else. I'd rather believe in Jesus as Messiah, and risk being wrong, than *not* believe and risk being wrong.

Nicodemus is almost there—how about you? Will you continue on your path of unbelief, risking your eternal destiny? Or will you choose to risk all in *this* life to follow the One Who holds that destiny in His hands. Your answer is the one which angels and all of heaven lean in to hear.

"Where are you going, husband?" Miriam asked Nicodemus. "It's late, and we should be in bed." Her eyes spoke the worry in her mind.

He had hoped to slip out after she was asleep, but she was still not feeling well and often had difficulty falling asleep.

"Council business," he said, more abruptly than he wished.

Miriam didn't say anything, just turned and walked back into their sleeping room. He followed her in, caught her by the shoulder, and turned her to face him. Her hurt expression stabbed him. *How I love this woman!*

"I'm sorry, Miriam. I didn't mean to be rude. It's just that Liam has a bee in his bonnet about this prophet, the Baptizer. I don't want to go, but he's called a meeting—again. Better that I placate him than ignore him, don't you think?" Nicodemus hated to lie, but he had to protect her, give the ruling council no reason to interrogate her.

Tiredly, Miriam said, "I suppose so. How I wish we could just be left alone and not be involved in all of this political intrigue!" She paused, then looked up into his face, her expression softer than before.

"Please, husband, be careful! There are always ne'er-dowells and ruffians on the streets at this time of night, especially during Passover."

Nicodemus leaned down and kissed the tip of her nose, then turned her around and gave her a playful push.

"Yes, my dear one, I will be careful. I will take my knife with me and brandish it at any challenger. Will that set your mind at ease?" Nicodemus saw her shoulders stiffen and knew he'd gone too far. Robberies and assaults during feast days in Jerusalem were sometimes vicious.

Nicodemus hastily apologized for teasing her, and giving her a last tight hug, walked out of their small home into the dark of the night. Nicodemus noted the stars were invisible and even the moon was just a sliver. *So much the better,* he thought as he took a last backward glance at his home. He was grateful to see the lamp in the window go out, as presumably Miriam went back to bed. He turned the corner at the end of their street and headed south.

***

The darkness of the night shrouded Nicodemus as he made his way through the narrow streets. He'd discovered where Jesus of Nazareth was staying, in a little house on the outskirts of the Lower City, which would mean a longish walk for him—especially since he'd plotted a circuitous route to get there. If he was noticed, which was unlikely at this time of night, he could claim he couldn't sleep and was taking a walk. There were still a few Passover revelers out in the streets, but they paid him no mind. An occasional shout could be heard in the distance, scuffling of feet in an alley, and the bleat of a sheep, but these did not have the power to break the concentration of Nicodemus's thoughts.

And what thoughts! He'd been taught the prophecies concerning Messiah since a boy at his father's knee, and now he reviewed them again, trying to find some reason to discount the possibility that Jesus of Nazareth was Messiah. But the more he recalled, the more convinced he became. As he walked, blanketed in the velvet night, with the prophecies engraved on the tablet of his mind, his heart told him Messiah had come.

What news! But news he could not share with the council and expect to live long. As a Pharisee, Nicodemus knew the dangerous precipice he walked—on the one side, perfect keeping of the law, and on the other side, wondering if the fulfiller of that law walked these streets on human feet.

No, the council does not want to hear this news; nay, perhaps they do want to hear it so those feet can be stopped. Their way of life, their livelihoods, their status among the peasants was threatened, and Liam and the rest of the Sanhedrin will stand for no competition.

Nicodemus sighed. *It always came down to the fine points of power and money.*

He walked on, considering, arguing with himself—playing the prosecutor and defender—until he turned a corner and his destination arose in front of him. The house was tiny, set back on the street, with a small porch overhung by the thatched roof. Everything was dark, only a tiny light glowing from a small window. Nicodemus judged it to be about four hours before dawn. As he came to within ten yards of the porch, he stopped abruptly, astonished at what he saw.

In the darkness, he could make out the dim outline of a man sitting on the porch. The man did not speak, but Nicodemus, moving closer, could see that the man stared in his direction. Nicodemus had a moment of intense fright, thinking this might be Liam or one of the council—perhaps they'd somehow discovered his plan to come tonight and speak to Jesus! But then he realized this was not so. It was Jesus of Nazareth himself. There was another chair placed next to Jesus, as if he was expecting company.

Into the blackness surrounding them, Jesus spoke. "Will you sit with me, my friend?"

Nicodemus couldn't find his voice. The thought that this man might be Messiah, that Messiah's audible voice spoke to him in the night, threatened to put him on his knees.

Jesus spoke again, gently. "I knew you would come tonight.

That's why I'm sitting here when we both should be sleeping. Please come and sit." His tone sounded almost playful to Nicodemus.

His brain finally convinced his feet to move, and he stepped up to the porch and sat down heavily in the chair. He still could not find his voice, and they sat in companionable silence for the next few minutes, the look of utter peace on Jesus's face contrasting with the turmoil Nicodemus knew must be etched on his own.

"My friend, whom do you seek?" Jesus whispered to Nicodemus after a few minutes of complete silence.

Nicodemus dared to lift his eyes to Jesus's face. He didn't know where to start—his questions fled his mind like the scattering of leaves in a strong wind. He said nothing.

"Nicodemus, whom do you seek?"

The use of his name brought all those questions rushing back to his mind, as if that strong wind had suddenly reversed direction.

"How do you know my name? I did not tell you!" Nicodemus challenged, raising his voice.

Jesus smiled and replied quietly, "Is that what you came to ask me—how I know your name?"

This was not going as he'd planned. Perplexed, Nicodemus started again.

"Rabbi," he said, remembering to lower his voice to a whisper, "we all know that God has sent you to teach us. Your miraculous signs are evidence that God is with you."

He paused to allow Jesus to answer clearly who he was. Nicodemus waited expectantly for that very declaration. *Messiah or no?*

Jesus replied, "I tell you the truth, unless you are born again, you cannot see the kingdom of God."

Once again, Nicodemus was confused. *He did not reveal who he is—his words say more about me than himself!*

Nicodemus turned Jesus's statement over in his logical mind. It challenged all his powers of intellect and reason; it challenged nature itself. He found himself echoing Liam's earlier disbelief. *Born twice? What utter nonsense!*

Nicodemus wasn't ready to give up yet, however—he vowed to keep an open mind, unlike Liam.

Jesus waited patiently, a look of intense anticipation on his face as Nicodemus considered.

"What do you mean?" Nicodemus finally asked, his voice rising in frustration. He then leaned closer to Jesus, whispering again, "How can an old man go back into his mother's womb and be born again?"

His question should have turned the tide of the conversation, since what was suggested was plainly impossible. But it didn't have the effect he'd anticipated—Jesus wasn't stymied at all by it. Nicodemus had a startling thought. *It's as if he knew I would ask it—as if my questions are already known to him—and he's been waiting to answer them.* The thought sent chills down his spine.

"You are a plain-speaking man, Nicodemus, and I will answer you plainly," Jesus said. "I've known you and loved you from the foundations of this world, and I know you to be an honest seeker, not one with an agenda. You are as unlike Liam as you can be—now *there's* one who deserves to lose his turban," he said with a chuckle.

Dumbfounded, Nicodemus was mute.

Jesus laid his hand on Nicodemus's arm and said, "Let me go on, if I may?"

Nicodemus nodded his assent, more confused than ever. But in the back of his mind, conviction was growing—conviction that shouted the truth about this man, Jesus of Nazareth—that he was no ordinary man.

"I assure you," Jesus said, "no one can enter the kingdom of God without being born of water and the Spirit."

Nicodemus was reminded of the words of John the Baptizer just hours ago.

"Humans can reproduce only human life," Jesus continued, "but the Holy Spirit gives birth to spiritual life. So don't be surprised when I say, 'You must be born again.' The wind blows wherever it wants. Just as you can hear the wind but can't tell where it comes from or where it is going, so you can't explain how people are born of the Spirit."

"How are these things possible?" Nicodemus asked.

Jesus looked amused at the question, some secret knowledge in his eyes. He murmured something under his breath that Nicodemus barely caught.

"So like Mother's question to the angel..." His voice trailed off into silence.

Nicodemus had no idea what Jesus was talking about. He asked his question again.

"Rabbi, how are these things possible?"

The question roused Jesus out of his intense contemplations.

"My friend, you are a respected Jewish teacher, and yet you don't understand these things?"

Nicodemus reacted with an intensity of his own.

"Sir, as you said, I am a plain-speaking man, yet you speak in riddles—men crawling back into their mothers' wombs, the Holy Spirit of God giving birth—how am I to react to that?"

Jesus sat up straight and leaned closer to Nicodemus, their faces inches apart.

"I assure you," he whispered, eyes locked on Nicodemus's, "we tell you what we know and have seen, and yet you won't believe our testimony. But if you don't believe me when I tell you about earthly things, how can you possibly believe if I tell you about heavenly things? No one has ever gone to heaven and returned. But the Son of Man has come down from heaven."

Jesus stared at Nicodemus's face intently, clearly seeing the struggle there—and then the final realization as Nicodemus arrived at the only logical conclusion.

Nicodemus sagged back in his chair, completely overwhelmed. *There it is! The plain declaration I seek. Son of Man! Clearly a reference to his full humanity and his full deity.*

"I see, Nicodemus, you have traveled the seeker's road—and now you have been found. Let me tell you more. As Moses lifted up the bronze snake on a pole in the wilderness, so the Son of Man must be lifted up so that everyone who believes in him will have eternal life."

Nicodemus felt the tears well up in his eyes. *This man, sitting here knee to knee with me in this small hovel in Jerusalem, is Messiah! He's here! But now he's talking about dying on a pole so I will have eternal life – how can I grasp this?*

Jesus answered his thought. "Yes, my friend. You will understand. For this is how God loved the world: He gave his one and only Son, so that everyone who believes in him will not perish but have eternal life. God sent his Son into the world not to judge the world, but to save the world through him."

Nicodemus heard those words, and he understood them. *Isaiah and all the prophets spoke of the suffering servant, one who would carry our transgressions to a traitor's grave, one whose stripes would heal mine. This is Messiah – Joseph and I were right! I can't wait until I can see him and tell him.*

He was sobbing in earnest now. He recalled his thought just hours ago, when they set out on this mission. *Four hundred years of God's silence has indeed been broken!* He embraced that belief with all his heart and mind as Jesus patiently explained more, sitting next to him on a small porch in Jerusalem as dawn crested the horizon.

Nicodemus had a date with Holy God. He didn't understand why until he kept the appointment. All human souls who have ever lived on this earth, and who will yet live, have a divine appointment. It matters not whether you believe it – you *will* have that appointment.

Nicodemus and Joseph believed Jesus was Messiah while still walking in human skin. We know that because later in the Scriptures they both go to Pilate and beg for the body of Jesus to give him a proper burial. Joseph went so far as to use his own family's tomb – no small sacrifice in those days. They knew who He was, and they knew the prophecies about the resurrection.

I also have believed in Jesus Messiah in this life. God's Word says I and all other believers will live forever in our loving Redeemer's presence because of our choice to believe.

If you choose unbelief during this life, and you die in that unbelief, His Word says you *will* believe—on your knees before Him—in the next moment after death. But it will be too late for you. There will not be an opportunity for a do-over. There's no eternal Reset button, no Escape or Delete key, no Backspace, no way to "unlike" your decision. You will carry your rejection of Christ to the grave and into eternity with no possibility of escape.

If you reject your Creator, the One Who stepped out of eternity to take your place on the cross, you will spend eternity apart from Him, with the sure knowledge—circling round and round in your head forever—that you made the wrong choice.

Do you really want to risk that? I don't.

Father, thank You for Your provision for me in Messiah Jesus. Help me believe!

Study Questions—By Night

1. From your knowledge of the times, what did Nicodemus and John risk by believing Jesus of Nazareth was Messiah? What do you admire about Nicodemus? What do you admire about John? Can you relate to the confusion of the times over who John and Jesus really were? Are you confused? Will you ask God to clear up your confusion?
2. What do you think is the significance of Liam's turban falling off? Can you relate that incident to religion today?
3. What emotion is evoked in you as you picture Jesus cleansing the temple? Do you long for a similar cleansing in your heart—for Jesus to come in and throw out your idolatry, your rebellion, your hypocrisy, and your confusion—to send the god of this age packing? Do you long for an undivided heart? What will you do about it?
4. What are you willing to risk to seek answers to your questions about Messiah?
5. Will you determine, here and now, to be a voice to the next generation? Not a whimpering voice, not a politically correct voice, but a fearless megaphone shouting the truth with reckless abandon to those whom God has placed in your life. Will you be a John the Baptizer in your world?

Chapter 4
Living Water

If you only knew the gift God has for you and who you are speaking to, you would ask me, and I would give you living water.
—John 4:10

Hana stumbled wearily along the rocky path to the well. Stopping to rest, she put the large jug on the ground at her feet and gazed at the barren landscape. The valley stretched before her, drenched in shimmering heat as far as her eyes could see.

Hot and dry, the narrow path wound gently down the rolling hillside, ending at the well. Sychar was behind her, a distance of about a mile. Walking this path twice a day had become more difficult with each passing year.

She contemplated the emptiness of the desert before her—mirroring the emptiness of her life. She no longer had to walk this path twice a day, for she had been told in no uncertain terms by the women of Sychar that she was not welcome anymore at their morning and evening gatherings. She was not welcome in the twice-daily gossip sessions, sharing stories of their children, or the womanly fellowship indulged in without listening male ears. She was relegated to getting water at noon, an absurd time to have to draw from the well.

She missed the gatherings though, more intensely than she'd thought possible. That day she'd been cornered in the street and told not to appear at the usual time, she'd stiffened her back and shoulders and walked away, trying to show those self-righteous women how much she didn't care. They'd called her a half-breed Samaritan whore. Remembering now, it brought hot tears to her eyes. *What do they expect from me?*

They called her a whore, although all five of her husbands were *husbands*! She'd been married five times per the custom of the day, setting up housekeeping without benefit of a legal ceremony. Most people did it that way, for there was no temple, no holy men in the area, and if there did happen to be one visiting, he wouldn't be concerned with marrying people—only collecting taxes. Her four previous husbands had either died or left her, so what did these women expect from her—to go through her entire life with no man to help her? She shuddered now, just contemplating the hardness of her life now with a husband—let alone without one.

As she bent down to pick up her water jug, heaving it to her shoulder, she stiffened the spine of her soul once again to put one foot in front of the other and tend to her duties. She repeated her mantra again, *I don't care. They can think what they like – I don't care.*

The familiar story of Jesus and the Samaritan woman at the well is found in John 4:1–42.

This woman was the product of generations of intermarriage between the conquered remnant of Israelites and their Assyrian occupiers, sent from Babylonia, Cutha, Ava, Hamath, and Sepharvaim to inhabit Samaria in order to maintain the peace and productivity of the area. They brought with them their own customs and religions, eventually mixing worship of their gods with worship of the God of Israel. They even constructed a temple on nearby Mount Gerizim that rivaled the Jerusalem temple, the only place pure Israelites would worship God.

The people of Samaria were hated and ostracized by the Jews for many reasons. During the time of Nehemiah and Ezra, after the Israelites gained the chance to return to their homeland, the foreign occupiers tried to stop the rebuilding of the wall of Jerusalem, and they were actually successful at halting the rebuilding of the temple for a time.

Under Sanballat, the leader of Samaria, and his son, who was installed as priest, the temple at Mount Gerizim became the recognized place of worship. The Samaritans believed it had been designated by Moses as the only place to worship God. This was a serious affront to the Israelites—the temple in Jerusalem was built by their ancestors and was the place where God dwelt.

To further cement the hostilities, Samaria had become a place of refuge for all the outlaws of Judea. Jewish criminals fleeing from justice were willingly received by the Samaritans. Violators of Jewish laws found safety for themselves in Samaria, greatly increasing the hatred that existed between the two nations.

In addition to all of the above, the Samaritans would only accept the five books of Moses and rejected the writings of the prophets and all the ancient Jewish traditions.

By the time of Jesus's day, the temple at Mount Gerizim had been destroyed, and the once large and thriving city of Sychar was only a small village.

Into this backdrop of suspicion, hatred, and division steps a woman with an unsavory past. She has three strikes against her—she's a half-breed Samaritan; she's a woman; and she has had several husbands, something frowned upon in polite Jewish society. The Bible doesn't tell us under what circumstances these five husbands had come to her or if she had actually been legally married to any of them. Jesus, in His conversation with her, hints at the truth.

Some scholars have attempted a correlation between the five husbands and the five nations that were sent to occupy Samaria; indeed, these scholars have drawn symbolism from this notion. The woman symbolizes Samaria, the five husbands represent the five occupying nations, and her present "husband" stood for the Samaritan religion.

But where we must settle our thoughts is that she is walking to get water for her household, an everyday task done in the ordinary, everyday way—but what she encounters is the promise of an entirely different kind of water offered in a spectacularly unordinary way.

Divine appointments are sometimes like that, coming to us when we least expect it, when we're just going about our business. God invades our space and turns the world upside down, and nothing is ever the same again.

Hana arrived at the stone well and sat down on the edge of it to catch her breath. Lately, she'd been feeling a sharp pain in her chest with exertion. She tried to ignore it—*after all, I'm not as young as I once was.* As she sat there, she looked out at the harsh desert, the foothills in the distance, and strained to hear the call of an eagle flying high in the sky above her. Shading her eyes, she looked up at the soaring eagle.

She watched for several minutes, enjoying the way the huge bird glided effortlessly one way, then suddenly wheeling around to fly in the opposite direction. He didn't seem taxed at all, using the unseen air currents to lift and drop him as he willed.

He came lower, circling the ground a few yards from her. She sat mesmerized, water forgotten.

If only life could be like that, she thought. *Lived effortlessly, floating high above the turmoil, above those who would harm, those who pointed, those who shamed without worrying about what was true or false. Ah, well, life is like that, and I'd best get on with it.*

The eagle had been circling lazily but suddenly dove, hurtling toward the earth at breakneck speed. Pulling up at the last possible moment, murderous talons extended downward in front of him, he clutched the small rabbit and swooped up again, all in one smooth movement. He made not a sound as he flew off, nor did the helpless animal he'd captured.

Beautiful life and cruel death, all in a blink. Hana knew with sudden clarity that she'd never be the eagle, soaring above the madness of this life. She would always be the rabbit—killed daily even while she lived—by the self-righteous hatred swirling around her, rooted in an ancestry over which she had no control. Just like the rabbit, who couldn't help what it was, she was doomed to go through life cowering, hiding, ever watchful, ever on guard against those who would try to destroy her. And she *did* care. She knew it now—she cared deeply.

Hana snapped out of her reverie as she spied the eagle gliding quickly out of sight with his next meal. She stood, stretching a moment, feeling the lessening of the pain in her chest. Taking the large pouch from around her waist, she hooked it to the rope dangling into the well and let the pouch down; it hit the water with a splash. Letting it sink and fill, she then started pulling it up. She strained, feeling the muscles in her arms, neck, and back pull.

Finally, the pouch was close enough for her to grab. She lifted it with just a bit more trouble than she had yesterday—each day was just a little harder. She poured the water into her jug, unhooked the pouch from the rope, and placed it around her waist again. She carefully lifted the jug to her shoulder and began the steep walk from the well to higher ground and the path back to Sychar.

What will happen when I'm too old and weak to get my own water? Who will help me? As she walked the mile or so back to Sychar, the familiar thoughts went round in her head. *What will happen when I'm too old? I have no children to care for me, and he who I call my husband is older yet than I. What will happen to me?*

In Hana's mind, even though she has a man in her life, she's entirely alone. Are there times when you feel the same?

We've heard it said that growing old is not for wimps. From the wrong side of sixty, I know this to be true. I'm standing at the edge of that cliff, looking over the scary precipice of age, and wondering some things.

Who will care for me? *He covers me with His feathers* (Psalm 91:4).

Will I have enough money to live on? *He carries me on eagles' wings* (Isaiah 40:31).

What if I get sick? *He heals all my diseases* (Psalm 103:3).

Can we keep these promises, and more, in mind as we slog through the mud of this world, aging a little more each day—each day just a little harder to get through?

We must keep it in mind, for each day brings us another opportunity to hear from God, to take the hand of another and help him or her along, to look upward and see the glory that awaits us.

And there just might be one of those divine appointments waiting around the corner of today that we dare not miss.

Early the next day, Hana made her way to the market. She always went early so as to avoid the townspeople. But for some reason, the streets this morning were more crowded than usual.

She sighed, noting the clusters of women laughing, talking, gossiping, close knit as only in a small town. She'd never be included with them. She knew there were other women, half-breeds like herself, who were ostracized from the community, but she had those two other strikes against her—her marital history and that, despite her age, she was still strikingly beautiful. Jealousy was a powerful obstacle to overcome, especially among women.

Hana avoided the chattering women, some of whom glared

her way.

What are they talking about, I wonder? What has happened to excite everyone so?

She came to the potter's stall, intending to buy a smaller water jug. It was getting more and more difficult to lift the one she had, and she'd spotted a small crack near the bottom. So after mentioning it to her husband, he'd given her a little extra coin to buy a new one. She'd brought the old one, thinking that even with the crack in it, she might be able to trade it to offset the price of a new one.

The potter refused to trade the old jug. Looking her up and down, he said, "I don't want used merchandise."

Cheeks reddening at his rudeness, she paid what he asked for, then remarked casually, trying to dispel the shame he'd cast upon her, "It seems that everyone is excited about something today."

He let down his reserve a little, no doubt wanting her to know that *he* knew something the half-breed didn't.

"So you obviously didn't hear the news, woman," he said haughtily. "Well, why would you? We have a visitor to the town. He arrived last night."

"Oh? Is that all?"

"Is that all? He is Jesus of Nazareth, woman! The same who has the whole region stirred up. *Is that all?*" he said in disgust. "Now go away, woman. I have other customers to tend to."

Hana had heard the name Jesus of Nazareth before. She'd overheard her husband and other men talk about him, but when she'd asked her husband about him, he'd given her a cuff on the head and told her to mind her own business and that it wasn't a subject she, an ignorant woman, needed to know about.

As she made her way home with her purchases, she wondered at the potter's words—*the same who has the whole region stirred up.*

Well, she thought now, *What has everyone stirred up? We've had many Jewish visitors to the region. What's different about this one?*

As Hana turned a corner in the street and headed across a small alley, she saw a sudden movement in the dim light between the buildings.

"Rachel? What are you doing here?" she asked, hurrying to her friend's side. Rachel was crouched on the ground, leaning sideways against the rough wall, hands covering her face. She tipped her head almost to the ground between her knees.

"Rachel," Hana said gently, bending down and patting her head. "Talk to me."

Rachel lowered her hands and looked up at Hana through eyes bruised and swollen. Hana gasped. The violent bruising looked obscene on her dainty features. She knelt beside the distraught young woman.

"Rachel, what happened to you?"

The young woman lowered her head again, sobbing.

"Rachel? Here, you must not give way, girl! Tell me at once," Hana demanded. She stood and helped Rachel up.

"It was that innkeeper, Hana," she said, struggling to her feet. She was smaller than Hana, barely reaching Hana's shoulder.

"He thought I was soliciting his guests—but I wasn't, Hana. I wasn't! I just wanted to work. My…my father threw me out two days ago, told me he couldn't feed me anymore, and it was time I found my own way." Rachel broke down and sobbed.

"What am I to do, Hana?" she pleaded.

Hana carefully placed her purchases at her feet and gathered Rachel into her arms. Rachel felt like a feather, flimsy and breakable.

"Oh, Hana, I miss my mother so! She'd never have let Father do this to me—I know she wouldn't. And he didn't throw my brothers out. I guess he has no trouble feeding them, yet I can hardly match their appetites!"

Hana nodded sadly, thinking to be born a woman was the first obstacle in this life to overcome. *Whatever gods governed the lives of men spared no thought for the women who'd birthed and cared for them.*

Rachel finally ceased sobbing and stepped back from Hana. Her face looked ravaged, red from weeping, eyes now almost swollen shut, the bruising now seeping over her cheekbones. Hana tenderly tucked a lock of hair behind Rachel's ear and smoothed her brow.

"I don't know what to do, Rachel. Perhaps I can ask Ahira if you can stay with us until we think of something," Hana suggested weakly. The women looked at each other, hope clearly springing in Rachel's face. It died quickly though at Hana's next words.

"I'm not sure though, Rachel. I can ask, but his mood hasn't been the best recently."

"Oh, Hana, don't ask him—I don't want to cause you any trouble with him," Rachel said glumly. She'd been witness to Ahira's abuse of Hana more than once.

"Well, I'd better get home. I should have been there by now, and he'll be wondering where I am." Hana paused, worry clearly lining her face.

Rachel squared her shoulders and drew herself up in an obvious attempt to ease that worry.

"Hana, you go home. I'll be fine. I'll figure something out," she said firmly. She paused, then reached for Hana's hand.

"Hana, have you heard of the one called the Teacher? He who goes around with a group of followers teaching about God?"

Hana was surprised. "Yes, I've heard something about him. Why?"

"Oh, nothing really. It's just that I heard he...he heals people, and he's kind to everyone—even women. I heard from my cousin that the Baptizer spoke of him, that when he baptized the Teacher in the Jordan, a dove from heaven came and sat on his shoulder."

"Oh, Rachel. Why are you listening to rumors? He's a Jew! Why would he ever be kind to women? All I've heard is this: he's a troublemaker, a heretic. You'd best not get your hopes up from that quarter, my girl," Hana said, more severely than she intended.

Rachel nodded, eyes on her feet, shoulders bowed again.

"All right, I really must go now," Hana said, bending to pick up her groceries. "I want you to call on me tomorrow though, after Ahira goes to his shop. Perhaps we can come up with a good plan then."

Rachel nodded and then turned and walked away, deeper into the alley. Hana watched her for a moment, anger at her friend's plight rising in her chest. She waited until Rachel turned a corner and disappeared.

Arriving home, she entered her small house and found her husband on the back porch instead of at work in the small carpentry shop he ran next to their home. Several men surrounded him. They talked heatedly, voices raised, arms waving, heads wagging. She quietly laid her items down on the table and crept closer to the open doorway to listen, unnoticed by the men.

"Ahira, are you saying you believe his teaching, what his followers have said?" asked one of the men. "Jesus of Nazareth is a troublemaker, surrounding himself with illiterate rabble-rousers. Our religious leaders have commanded us to have nothing to do with him. Tell me you're not taken in by his heresies!"

Her husband answered vehemently.

"No, of course not! I'm just saying there must be a reason he's here! Why would a Jew not circumvent this area like they all do? They say he's on his way home to Galilee. Why would he stop here? What would bring him here?" Ahira challenged.

"Well, who really cares? The problem is that he's a heretic by all accounts, and now our women are gabbling about him, asking questions. You know how women are—always grasping at the latest gossip, gullible, looking for miracle cures to their ailments. Ahira, we must not give any sort of credence to this fellow, lest our women be swayed."

"Of course I agree," Ahira said, clearly trying to downplay his interest. "I was just curious, that's all. Jews don't usually come here unless they have business, and so far, he doesn't seem to have met with anyone. He just stayed outside the town, sleeping on the ground last night with those followers of his. It's mysterious to me, that's all. No need to get all up in arms over it, my friends."

After murmuring assent all around, the conversation ended. Hana hurried away from the doorway, not wishing to be caught eavesdropping. The men drifted out the side door of the porch and went their way. Ahira came in through the back door, brow furrowed in thought. He saw her immediately.

Clearly suspicious, he demanded, "And how long have you been home?"

"Just got back," she answered quickly, "and see the new jug I have," she added, trying to divert his suspicion. She held it up.

"Hmm, and how much did he give you for the old one?"

Her face burned as she remembered the potter's remark. *Used merchandise.*

"Nothing—I had to pay the full price," she said, lowering her eyes to her feet in shame.

"That figures—women! I would have been able to talk him down," he said with a sneer. He hefted the new jug in his hands.

"This is so much smaller, Hana. You'll now need to make two trips at noon every day to get enough water. Seems like it won't help you at all—I thought the point was that you're having trouble making one trip with the jug you had. Now you'll be going twice."

"I was thinking, husband," she began timidly. "I was thinking maybe you could help me with it..." She got no further, stumbling back at the sudden suffusion of color in his face.

"What? Me, carry water like some weak female? It's women's work to carry water, Hana," he shouted. "Don't ever say that to me again, or you'll feel my anger across your pretty little face!" Ahira stalked out the front door.

She sagged against the table in relief. She could hear him out in his carpentry shop, banging with a hammer, probably on the first piece of wood he found. *At least he's not hitting me this time.*

She moved shakily to the table to put her purchases away and tidy their eating area, hands moving restlessly. His anger could flare suddenly at the least provocation. She'd spent the last five years trying to avoid those outbursts. She walked a thin line—between him, the hatred of the townspeople, and her own thoughts. *Maybe that's why I'm aging so fast,* she thought now.

She remembered the eagle and the rabbit, and tears welled just behind her eyelids, spilling over her cheeks. *Always the rabbit.*

***

Two hours later, in the hour before noon, word came to Hana from a neighbor that Rachel's body had been found just south of Sychar, between the village and Mount Gerizim, beaten and bloodied, the sacrifice she'd been carrying to offer to the gods scattered over her lifeless form. Hana was mute, unable to speak. She watched, tearless, as her neighbor backed away from her, turned, and fled. She stood motionless for long moments, unfocused, as life in Sychar flowed past her unseeing eyes.

Ah, well, the suffering of this life can't touch her anymore. Pray the gods she is at peace now, past the violence, out of reach of the eagle, no longer the rabbit.

Rousing herself from her silent grief, Hana prepared Ahira's midday meal, knowing he'd be demanding it soon. Working quickly, she forced the vision of Rachel's lifeless body to the recesses of her mind—where dwelt the rabbit—in a place tucked away where she wouldn't have to think on it.

***

At noon she made the tiresome journey to Jacob's well again. The smaller jug was much easier to handle, but knowing she'd have to make two trips caused her to wish she still had the larger one. It had been heavy, but at least the path to the well only had to be trod once a day. Each step she took seemed harder knowing that, and the memory of the scorn on her husband's face made it worse.

She stopped halfway there and sat down on a large rock along the path. Again, the landscape was completely empty, the sun scorching her head covering.

She looked for the eagle and strained to hear his cry, but nothing moved in the sky today except a few wispy clouds. She was completely alone in this wide desert—the wide desert of her life.

After resting a few moments, she picked up the water jug, placed it on her shoulder, and trudged along the path again. She had to be careful here. The path narrowed, and she used to be able to navigate the rocky ground with ease, but now she must watch that she didn't stumble and fall.

She came to the place where the ground sloped down toward the well, situated in the center of a depression in the ground. She could see it in the distance, surrounded by large stones brought from the hillsides across the valley. Stopping to rest again, her thoughts circled restlessly, as the eagle had over its prey the day before.

Hana remembered the stories of their father Jacob, who purchased the property on which the well sat. He gave one hundred pieces of silver—in Hana's mind an exorbitant amount of money. Jacob had built an altar to God at this place and named it El-Elohe-Israel.

Mighty is the god of Israel? Perhaps in Jacob's time, or further back in Abraham's time, but now, today, where is this mighty god? Does this god live in the scornful faces of the "pure" Israelites who point their fingers at me and call me a half-breed whore?

Where was he when I was born, and no sooner was I given into my mother's arms than she breathed her last? Where was he when my father turned me out, unable to look at my face because I killed with my birth the woman he loved? Where was he when I ate scraps on the garbage heap outside of town? And when the first man took me, leav-

ing me sobbing in an alley? And where were you today, when Rachel…when Rachel lay dying alone in a pool of her own blood, holding in her hand the sacrifice brought to appease your wrath? Where were you then?

Hana sighed, put these thoughts away from her, and continued down the path. It would serve no purpose to give in to that despair again. She must get her water and go home to serve Ahira his midday meal. She must not be late.

As she approached the well, she was surprised to see a man sitting on a large rock next to it. She stopped in her tracks, not knowing what to do. She was unused to seeing anyone at the well at this time of day—and a man? How could she go down there? From the look of him, judging by the fringe on his dusty cloak, he was an Israelite. For her to even approach him to get her water would be a serious affront to his Jewish dignity.

She needed water, but now she was afraid. The consequences of coming near him, out here alone in the desert, could be severe. The vision of Rachel's body lying swollen and bloody in the wilderness arose unbidden. She agonized, sweating in her fear.

I'm the rabbit, cowering in fear. The talons of Judaism are reaching out for me once again. But I need the water! I have to have the water—my husband will beat me if I come home without it.

Finally, after several moments of indecision, she bravely squared her shoulders and continued forward, stepping to within a few feet of the man. At first she thought he was asleep. He didn't move, sitting on the rock with his head lowered until his chin rested on his chest. She set the jug down with trembling hands and took her leather pouch from around her waist. She moved quietly, deliberately, hoping not to disturb the man.

As she was hooking the pouch to the rope, the man spoke.

"Please give me a drink," he said, rasping out the words through dry, cracked lips.

Startled, she had to grasp the pouch tightly to keep from dropping it into the well.

She twisted around to look closely at him. He was indeed an

Israelite. He looked exhausted. His face was smudged with dirt. His hands were large and calloused. Letting her eyes travel up to his face, expecting to see scorn in his eyes, she was surprised to see kindly interest. Still, she must be on her guard. It could be a ruse to see if she would break Israelite law.

"You are a Jew, and I am a Samaritan woman," she said politely. "Why are you asking me for a drink?"

It seemed a natural question, but now her boldness made her nervous. Perhaps she shouldn't have spoken. If she were in the town, with others around to witness, she would have received a cuff on her head, or worse, for speaking to a Jewish man—even if he was the one who started the conversation. She waited, trembling, for his answer.

"If you only knew the gift God has for you and who you are speaking to, you would ask me, and I would give you living water," he replied.

Hana's practical mind completely ignored almost everything he'd said and focused instead on what she observed.

"But, sir, you don't have a rope or a bucket," she said, "and this well is very deep. Where would you get this living water?"

The man said nothing.

Living water? What does he mean? I need real water.

The man still said nothing, eyes probing hers gently.

It's as if he knows my questions.

"And besides, sir," she began, "do you think you're greater than our ancestor Jacob, who gave us this well, El-Elohe-Israel?"

It was a brazen question, one for which she should have been severely chastised, but the man merely gazed at her. She gathered her courage.

"How can you offer better water than Jacob and his sons and his animals enjoyed?"

She was rewarded by a wide smile on the man's face, encompassing not only his mouth but his whole face, lighting his eyes and crinkling his forehead.

The man replied gently, standing to his feet and spreading

his arms to encompass the entire empty desert landscape. "Anyone who drinks *this* water will soon become thirsty again. But those who drink the water I give will never be thirsty again. It becomes a fresh, bubbling spring within them, giving them eternal life." His voice seemed part of the sky, the solid earth on which they both stood, even the air she breathed.

With an almost physical shock to her mind, Hana understood who this man was.

It must be he whom everyone was talking about, whom my husband and his friends were talking about—Jesus of Nazareth. Why is he sitting out here all alone?

Again, he answered her unspoken question.

"I'm out here waiting for you, for I knew you'd come," he said gently. Then he turned from her, leaving her mind and heart tumbling out of control.

The man sat down again, gazing outward at the dry hills beyond the desert. Hana found she was not uncomfortable with the silence between them.

Eternal life? Never thirst again?

As the words presented themselves to her, the man turned again and looked at her.

"Yes, my dear? You wish to ask me something?"

The words rushed out of her mouth like a creek swollen from the spring rains—she had no control over them. She only knew how urgently she wanted *his* water.

"Please, sir," Hana said desperately, moving a pace toward him, eyes pleading, "please give me this water! Then I'll never be thirsty again, and I won't have to struggle here every day to get water."

He answered her, but not her plea.

"Go," he said, "and get your husband."

As he spoke, she heard the eagle's cry in the distance—and there arose in her mind the vision of his talons extended, grasping the innocent rabbit, the limp body carried away.

"No, Hana, don't be afraid," he said simply, stepping to her side and touching her hand.

It so alarmed her to be touched by this man, a Jew, that the vision fled just as the eagle had flown away. She bowed her head as she tucked her hand behind her.

"I don't have a husband," she said quietly, eyes downcast in shame, for she knew the truth. The man was correct.

"You're right!" he exclaimed. "You don't have a husband—for you have had five husbands, and you aren't even married to the man you're living with now."

His voice, ever so tender, spoke the words she needed to hear, needed to grasp.

"Hana, you certainly spoke the truth."

"Sir, how do you know my name? We have never met—and I don't know yours!"

"My name is Jesus of Nazareth. And I have known you and loved you since before your birth—and after, when you were laid in your dying mother's arms."

Hana was astonished. She didn't know what to make of him. He didn't resemble the man Ahira and his friends had spoken of on the porch earlier—the heretic, the troublemaker, the traitor. His words confused her.

"Sir," she said shyly, daring to lift her eyes to his, "you must be a prophet."

Jesus said nothing. The silence once again stretched between them.

Hana went on. "So tell me, why is it that you Jews insist that Jerusalem is the only place of worship, while we Samaritans claim it is here at Mount Gerizim, where our ancestors worshiped?"

Jesus smiled a little at her question, then turned his head away. The eagle had appeared in the distance, lazily floating high above. Hana thought she could hear Jesus saying something—his face pointed to the sky—but with his head away from her, she couldn't make out his words. They watched the eagle for a moment in companionable silence, and then Jesus turned back to face Hana.

"Yes, Hana, I am a prophet. You are correct in what you say.

I am a prophet, so I know completely what is in your heart today," he said. "To answer your question, I will say this. You must believe me, dear Hana, that the time is coming when it will no longer matter whether you worship the Father on this mountain or in Jerusalem."

Oh, he'd be wise to keep that to himself! This must be the heresy of which he is guilty.

"Yes, Hana, it is," Jesus replied, as if she'd spoken aloud.

"You Samaritans know very little about the one you worship, while we Jews know all about him, for salvation comes through the Jews," Jesus said.

"But, sir, don't we both worship the same god?" Hana asked.

Jesus answered her with a shake of his head, then continued his gentle instruction.

"But the time is coming—indeed it's here now—when true worshipers will worship the Father in spirit and in truth. The Father is looking for those who will worship him that way. For God is Spirit, so those who worship him must worship in spirit and in truth."

"I know the Messiah is coming—the one who is called Christ. When he comes, he will explain everything to us," Hana said eagerly.

The eagle cried again, and they both looked up. It was right above their heads, high in the sky.

Quietly, face uplifted to the sky, he said, "I AM the Messiah!"

The earth under her feet trembled, shifted. Hana felt behind her to steady herself against the stonework surrounding the well.

This man – Messiah! She searched his face and knew the truth.

She sat down hard, breath coming in great gasps. Jesus sat down next to her, gently taking her hand in his.

"Hana, you are no longer the rabbit. You are the eagle if you choose to follow me. Will you?"

She looked up at him then, locked her eyes on his, and knew in her heart he spoke the truth about everything, about her.

"Yes, I will, Lord," she said simply, settling the matter

between them forever.

Are you sitting at the well today, your well, once again trying to quench your thirst with your own pitiful water? Your water that will never completely satisfy? That water that gives you a tantalizing taste of pleasurable satiation but leaves you more thirsty than ever—but thirst for this world, not the next? That impotent water we draw for ourselves goes by many names:

money
power
Hollywood
me time
romance
self-esteem
prestige
stuff

This water is a vapor, lasting a mere moment, unable to satisfy but for a blink in time.

God promises to quench our thirst forever, making in us a spring of water always bubbling to the surface, able to completely satisfy and spill over to those around us. He speaks of the Holy Spirit, who inhabits us the moment we ask Him and never leaves, who provides help and hope without end.

That is the water Hana sought so desperately as she spoke with Jesus of Nazareth that day at the well. She came, weary, hopeless, and helpless, and left energized, full of hope, and empowered by the living water Jesus offered her. She chose living water from Him over the dry, dusty dregs from her own crumbling well.

Which water will you leave with today?

Just then, his disciples returned. Hana hadn't heard their approach, so intense was her focus on Jesus. They fanned out around them, clearly astonished that the Teacher was speaking with a Samaritan, and a woman at that. Hana thought a few looked as if they'd like to chastise him, but no one dared.

She turned her focus back on the face of Jesus, whose eyes had never left her. She read his expression and knew what she must do. Just thinking of the task that lay ahead gave her an intense fright. *Am I really the eagle?*

Jesus nodded his head slightly and glanced up the path toward the village. She settled.

"I…I must leave, sir," she stammered.

She left her water jug, unneeded now, on the ground beside the well and ran back toward Sychar.

***

Jesus saw the questions in the eyes of his disciples.

"She'll be back, my friends, and with others who need this living water," he said quietly.

"Lord, we brought food for you," one said, holding out a bag of bread and vegetables.

Jesus looked up, seeing the eagle, now flying in a straight line toward the distant foothills. He smiled.

"I have already eaten, my friends, food you know nothing about," he said with a chuckle.

The disciples looked at each other in obvious confusion, murmuring and scratching their heads.

"Simon, did you sneak back here with food for him?"

"No, of course not, Andrew. I was with you the whole time!"

"Well," James said, "who brought him food then? It wasn't me! And I know it wasn't you, Levi, because you were with me. So who was it?"

And they continued asking each other until Jesus finally held up his hand to silence them.

"My very good friends, my nourishment comes from doing the will of God, who sent me, and from finishing his work. And

I say to you now, you must wake up, because the fields are ripe for harvest," he said, looking at each in turn.

Just then there came the sound of a throng of people heading their way. They looked up and saw the people of Sychar, led by Hana, streaming down the path to the well.

"Indeed, my friends," Jesus said, standing to his feet, arms out in a welcome embrace, "the harvest is plenty and ripe, and here it comes. Hana has done the work I sent her to do."

When Hana reached Jesus, she dropped to her knees before him and bowed her head. "Well done, child," he said, warm hand on her head.

"Yes, no longer the rabbit," Jesus added to himself.

The Scriptures tell us that many people in Sychar believed in Jesus that day because of the bold witness of the half-breed, the woman with the unsavory past, who chose to throw in her lot with Jesus of Nazareth.

Her witness to them was simple: "He told me everything I ever did!"

And somehow those plain words reached the hearts of the very people who had shunned her. She spoke the words that God told her to speak and didn't try to make them eloquent or high sounding. She spoke from her heart and her past—and those she spoke to could see the change in her. No longer hiding, no longer cowering in shame, no longer afraid, she drew them in, giving them a thirst for this water she'd received from the hand of Messiah.

And what words has God given us to say? Do we speak eloquent words that sound nice, canned words emptied of meaning because they've been spoken by so many, words that have been applied so generally that they can be used in any circumstance without any commitment at all?

"Don't worry—God loves you!"

"God just wants everyone to be happy."

"Just follow your heart—that's all God expects you to do."

These words, although containing some infinitesimal element of truth, won't lead anyone to the living water Jesus offers.

We must speak from our hearts, from God's sometimes bitter dealings with us, if we would lead others to this living water. We must speak from the vantage point of the keen-sighted eagle, flying high above the earth, where we can see our lives through God's eyes. In God's economy, *nothing* is wasted—of blessings, hurts, betrayals, of the harshness of life in the shadowlands. These are the framework of the message God has given us.

Do you have a past of which you're not proud? I do. Speak of it! Encourage another guilt-ridden soul to believe that even *this* can be forgiven.

Have you lost a child to drugs, alcohol, or death? Speak of it! Lead another to the living water that heals all wounds.

Have you made poor financial decisions that have limited your present opportunities? Speak of it! Help others to make right decisions, decisions that will widen their giving opportunities.

Are you enduring the pain of disease ravaging your body, day following weary day, endless treatments, visits to yet another specialist saying words of encouragement that sound suspiciously false? Speak of it! *Be* that living water springing up in order to help another along the grace-filled path you now walk.

Have you experienced that loss of losses, the death of your lifetime mate, the spouse God graciously gave to you and then took away? Speak of it! Don't be silent about the intense pain, the nights reaching across the empty bed, the times you speak a thought or a question, forgetting it's to an empty room. Speak of God's mercy toward you, His life-giving water as you now navigate life alone. You might just be the instrument of another's healing.

We must speak life-giving words—words from the living water within us. God has promised to put those words in our mouths. Hana said the words God gave her, simple words, and many believed.

What words has God given you to say? Who has He placed in your path—who in your life today needs this living water?

Father, please help me to speak from my life in order to draw others to Your water, the water that quenches eternally. Amen.

Study Questions — Living Water

1. In what ways do you identify with Hana?
2. Describe, in your own words, how the water of this life has left you unquenched.
3. Hana compared her life to that of the rabbit. She longed to be the eagle. To what do you compare your life? The rabbit, the eagle, or something else entirely?
4. The eagle's talons symbolized the grip of Judaism, creating a lifeless religion. What grips you today, rendering you helpless to draw from the spring of living water offered to you by Messiah?
5. Are you still drawing water from your own well — that water that will never satisfy completely? Or have you come to Jesus for living water, His Spirit, who quenches eternally your thirst for relationship with El-Elohe-Israel?

Chapter 5
The Tree

For the love of money is the root of all kinds of evil. And some people, craving money, have wandered from the true faith and pierced themselves with many sorrows.

—1 Timothy 6:10

He ran as fast as his short legs would carry him. He had always been fast, but now it was doubly important—the boys chasing him gained on him. If he couldn't get away, he'd have to endure another beating.

He rounded a corner, spied the tree, and sprinted toward it. Trees were the safest place for him. He'd found refuge in this one many times before. Scrambling up, he barely got himself hidden in its massive branches before the ruffians barreled around the corner.

He grinned as they looked this way and that, scratched their heads, shrugged, and disappeared the way they'd come. *Whew! Another drubbing avoided. Sometimes it's better to be small, fast, and smart than big, slow, and stupid.*

Zacchaeus waited a full thirty minutes before climbing down, carefully carrying the carved figure of a Roman soldier he'd appropriated from one of the boys—which was the reason for the chase. They didn't know for sure it'd been him. They hadn't seen him take it. It had been just pure bad luck that one of them had seen him in the vicinity of their play and assumed it was him. He was confident they would not come after him again—for this anyway. They would soon forget the affront and move on to some other poor kid to pick on. It was always the same in Jericho—nothing much ever changed in the City of Palms.

He had acquired a reputation, even at the tender age of twelve, of being a thief and a cheat. He was the despair of his mother and his older sister. And his father—now there was a man who had a permanent scowl on his face whenever he looked at his son. He constantly reminded his son that as a descendant of Abraham, he had a responsibility to be honest, to learn the ways of Yahweh, and to follow the Torah. Whippings were commonplace, something Zacchaeus endured without much remorse.

But Zacchaeus had learned something in his short life, learned it by observing the adults around him. Everybody cheated. Everybody lied. And the only way to get ahead was to take what you wanted. The Romans took his father's money, exacting inflated taxes from his balsam exportation business. The priests raised the payment for forgiveness almost daily. Even healing had its price—*what a racket!*

The way Zacchaeus saw it, you were either on the side of getting rich or on the side of getting poor. There didn't seem to be any in-between. And he'd already decided which side he wanted to be on.

Tucking the toy into his outer cloak, he strolled around the side of the small home he shared with his parents and sauntered off down the street to find some gullible child to sell it to—*and, of course, for far more than it's worth!*

Fast-forward a couple of decades and meet the grown up Zacchaeus, striding through the streets of Jericho with his scrolls and coin bag, still small, still a cheat, but now under the protection of the Roman government. People still look down on his short stature, but they dare not interfere with him in his tax-collection booth.

The Internal Revenue Service of the twenty-first century has nothing on Zacchaeus. He was a tax collector for Rome, schooled in the art as a young man, and sent back to his hometown to ply his trade.

We complain about paying taxes for everything from nonfood groceries to clothes, but in the time of Jesus, on the streets where his feet walked, people were charged for much more than groceries and clothing. They had to pay for cleansing. They had to pay for forgiveness. If they were sick, they had to pay for the prayers of the priest for healing. How would you like to walk in to your church for a worship service and have to pay for the privilege?

The IRS may be a hated institution, but tax collectors in the first century were reviled, shunned, sometimes attacked and brutalized.

They collected taxes—overcharging and cheating—with impunity because the more they collected from peasants and wealthy alike, the more their Roman masters could take.

Zacchaeus is just as hated now as he was when a boy. He is now a wealthy man, wealth made on the livelihoods of rich and poor alike. But into his life one day will walk a man who will show him true wealth, true strength, true courage.

And as always, when Jesus of Nazareth enters a life, nothing is ever the same again.

Hastening along the crowded street, his entourage surrounding him, Zacchaeus heard the faint hissing and saw the scowls. He was used to it, but it didn't bother him as long as they paid. Zacchaeus had learned his business of tax farming from the best, and he'd even surpassed his Roman mentor in the art of exacting payment down to the last *quadran* and *lepton* owed by the poorest of peasants. The years spent in Rome and Jerusalem learning his trade were not wasted. And now, posted back to Jericho to collect taxes from his hometown was just about perfect in his book.

Arriving at the place he intended to set up his booth, at a prime spot near the town square—reserved for the most elite publicans—he was disgruntled to see Moises sitting there.

Stopping, he took his assistant, Akim, who was also his cousin, by the arm. "Akim, go get rid of that idiot. Take two with you and throw him out—and make sure he knows whose spot that is," he ordered.

Akim was at least two heads taller than Zacchaeus and much broader, with thick muscles—a most imposing man, which was the principle reason Zacchaeus kept him around.

Moises was soon dispatched, minus his gold, which Zacchaeus thought was only fair. *He needs to learn, and soon, who is the chief tax collector in Jericho now. It's me, and no other. The sooner the other publicans learn that, the better.*

Soon, his booth was set up and he was in business. Another Passover season was approaching, with many opportunities to increase his usurious wealth by the townspeople he'd grown up with, by the very same boys—now grown—who'd amused themselves at his expense when they were children. And even more lucrative was the taxation of the visitors to the region, on their way to Jerusalem, who must exchange their godless foreign currency for acceptable coinage when visiting the temple. The rate of exchange Zacchaeus charged was at least twice what other publicans collected—but that was the perk of being the *chief* tax collector of Jericho. He could charge whatever he wanted and get away with it. It was well known that to wait until arriving at the Jerusalem temple risked an even higher rate, so many visitors stopped in Jericho first.

Zacchaeus felt very satisfied with himself. His conscience was quiet—he was doing what he knew to do, what he'd been trained to do. If others didn't like it, if they called him a lackey of Rome, a cheat and a liar—well, it was no more than what he'd grown up with. The difference now was his wealth. Watching the masses of poor people pass by, he told himself he was blessed. *So what if they weren't? It's not my fault they hadn't made more of themselves. Just as in ancient Jericho, the city was filled with Rahabs – irresolute sinners who freeloaded on decent society.* And so Zacchaeus comforted himself as he listened to the coins drop into his plates.

Later, after sunset, his assistants helped him pack up his booth. He paid them what they'd agreed to, and they went on their way. Only Akim would accompany him through the streets that had emptied, as the townspeople had finished their business and gone to their homes.

"A prosperous day, Zacchaeus?" Akim asked him as they strolled. Zacchaeus never imparted to Akim—or anyone else, for that matter—just how prosperous the day had been.

"Yes, somewhat, cousin. Of course, after I pay my tax to Rome, it will be less so. You have no idea how greedy they are, Akim. I'm living, but not as well as I could if not for the greed of the Roman government." Zacchaeus shook his head sadly while fingering the heavy bag of coin in the secret lining of his cloak.

"To hear you talk, Zacchaeus, I'm surprised you can pay me what you do," Akim said slyly. His point was not lost on Zacchaeus. Akim was fishing for just how much money he had.

Zacchaeus replied magnanimously, his chest puffed out, "Why, Akim, my most beloved cousin! Even if it put me in the poorhouse, I'd pay you what you're worth. Don't you worry about that. I'll always take care of you. I promised your dear mother the day she died that you would never want for anything." He shook his head, gazing solemnly at Akim.

"And do you, my dear Akim? Want, I mean?" he asked, pretending to look anxious.

"No, of course not, Zacchaeus," Akim said hastily. "You are most generous with me. I'm grateful to you, cousin, and my wife is grateful as well."

They fell silent for a moment, walking slowly through the streets, always with a wary eye for robbers lurking in the shadows of the buildings. They both carried long daggers with which to protect themselves—and the money Zacchaeus carried—should the need arise.

Zacchaeus broke the silence.

"Akim, what's this rumor I've heard about Levi?"

"Levi? Oh, you mean Matthew?"

"Whatever he calls himself these days," Zacchaeus replied impatiently. "Is it true he gave up his tax business to follow that traveling preacher?"

"That's what I heard! He must be as crazy as the one he follows," Akim replied. "Why do you think he'd do that? It makes no sense."

"You think I know?" Zacchaeus huffed disagreeably. "I always thought Levi was a little weak minded. He's always been a follower, from what I've heard, never an instigator, never a leader," Zacchaeus declared, insinuating that *he* wasn't at all cut from the same cloth as Levi.

Akim agreed. "Well, less competition is always good, I suppose. I just wish I understood the pull this Jesus of Nazareth—a lowly carpenter, mind you—has on the masses. His popularity is growing by leaps and bounds."

"Not with the rulers, Akim, not with the rulers," Zacchaeus said cryptically.

"What do you know that I don't? What do you mean, 'not with the rulers'?"

"Nothing, really. Just rumors and speculation as usual."

"Oh," Akim said, clearly disappointed that Zacchaeus wouldn't part with the dirt.

"I'm sure it's nothing, Akim. Now, what else have you heard?"

"I heard he claims to be a god, is able to make the desert bloom, conjure up lunch for thousands, and even raise the dead!" Akim waved his hands in excitement.

"Levi? Are you sure that's what you heard?"

Akim looked confused for a moment and then understood.

"No, I meant this carpenter from Nazareth!" Akim said impatiently.

"Oh...I thought...I thought you were talking about..."

Zacchaeus started, a devilish grin on his face.

Akim didn't let him get any further.

"Zacchaeus, you're teasing me! You know who I was talking about!"

"Okay, okay, yes I knew. But I was asking you about Levi—what else have you heard?"

Akim thought for a moment. "Well, I heard that when this Jesus called his name, he just got up from his tax booth and went after him. He left everything behind, even his collection plates with the coin still in them."

"You don't say! How curious—what would make a man do that?" Zacchaeus said, half to himself. He couldn't imagine leaving even half a shekel in one of his collection plates.

"I don't know. Perhaps this preacher has powers of persuasion and can so bemuse a man that he forgets himself and just follows him blindly," Akim responded.

"You know, you may be right about that. I've heard some things from Liam—you know, one of the rulers in Jerusalem. He told me quite some time ago, when I was posted there, about someone named John—another so-called prophet—and how John actually baptized this one called Jesus. Liam told me he met John on several occasions and that he was a blatant blasphemer," Zacchaeus said. "I guess it's only right he lost his head. Not that I care so much about religion, but still, it's curious that Levi is now following one who was baptized by a false prophet, don't you think?"

"Very curious, cousin. And something even more curious: I heard that Levi threw a party—killed the fatted calf, so to speak—on the very day he left his booth to follow the preacher. And he invited Jesus. And get this—Jesus actually went!" Akim drew out the story dramatically.

"You don't say...you don't say! A supposed holy man eating with a publican? If he were a god, why would he sully himself like that?" Zacchaeus said with a sneer.

"I don't know. I really don't know. But I heard it was the party of the year in that region. Everyone was invited, all of

Levi's friends, even people off the street went—and it lasted well into the night," Akim said, clearly as puzzled as Zacchaeus.

The two men had now arrived at Zacchaeus's home. Akim helped him stow his supplies in an attached shedlike structure next to the house, and then made ready to leave.

"Uh, Akim, do you want to come in for a meal?" Zacchaeus asked.

"Oh, no, I'm due at home…in fact, I'm a bit late as it is. I'm sure my wife is holding supper for me, and I must help her with the children. Thanks anyway though. I'll see you tomorrow, cousin." Akim backed down the path as he spoke.

Zacchaeus watched him walk quickly away, then turned and went inside, resigned to eating another meal alone.

As he prepared his solitary meal—having given his servant time off to attend a wedding—Zacchaeus's mind dwelt on the story of Jesus going to a party at Levi's house. He couldn't remember ever throwing a party at his own house. And if he did, he doubted anyone would come but people who wanted to ingratiate themselves—those who wanted something from him.

He sat at his table alone, eating in silence. He could hear the shouts of children outside in the street, parents calling them to come in, and the tinkling bells of sheep and goats in the distance. Inside his house it was so quiet he could hear the dripping of water from outside on the back porch. Too quiet.

What would it be like to throw a party and have people come and have a good time? What would it be like to have real friends, not those who always had their hands out? Even my own cousin is kept by me, dependent on me. Even he can't, or won't, stay and share a meal with me. What would it like to be taller, to not always have to look up to everyone else?

Zacchaeus didn't like where his thoughts led him. He pushed his feelings down somewhere inside himself, to the place he'd carved out when he was a child—a safe place, a place where no one but he could go.

His tree was there, the tree that had sheltered him as a child, provided refuge from bullies, from his father's scowl, from his isolation. The tree had grown larger in his mind as he had grown up, large enough to now hide from his secret, unfulfilled dreams—a wife, children, true friendship, respect—just as he'd hidden from the smaller problems of his childhood.

He could still see his childhood tree if he walked down a certain street in Jericho and stopped in front of a certain house—the house in which he'd grown up. But he preferred not to go *there*. He preferred the tree in his mind because it would never grow old and lose its leaves or become diseased and topple over. It flourished year after year, sheltering him when his chosen life disappointed him, or the people around him did, or his inadequacies reared their ugly heads.

He refused to allow those feelings out into the open. He refused to be a victim. He refused to admit his loneliness, even to himself. Instead, as he did now, he climbed the tree in his mind, nestled himself down among its green leaves and massive branches, and was comforted.

He told himself he was fine, his life was great, he had no need of friendships and fellowship, no need of parties and jollity. He repeated this over and over, willing himself to believe it. And as always, he fell asleep there in his tree, his mind righting itself in the knowledge that he was rich, massively rich, and he had no need of anyone or anything.

Jesus once said that it would be easier for a camel to walk through the eye of a needle than for a rich man to walk into the kingdom of God (Matthew 19:23). In another place, He said, "What sorrow awaits you who are rich, for you have your only happiness now." (Luke 6:24)

Jesus wasn't saying it's a sin to have wealth; He taught us that if we trust only in our wealth to make us happy, that will be the only happiness we will ever experience. The only way to walk into the kingdom of God is on our knees.

Most of us don't have exorbitant wealth to tangle us up. More often we have faith in ourselves, our accomplishments, maybe even in our religion to make us fit for heaven. We feel "wealthy" in these areas.

Zacchaeus has always taken refuge in his position and great wealth, but now he's plagued—more and more—by doubts. God is facing him with his need, with his lack, with that tree in his mind that will never be enough to provide the true refuge he craves. Creator God is doing what He does—creating an impending showdown—to help Zacchaeus see his need he didn't know was there.

There was a stir in Jericho the next day. As Zacchaeus left his home, he saw small groups of people standing in the street, talking excitedly, waving their arms, calling to their neighbors. He stood outside his home wondering what had happened, but no one paid him any mind. Zacchaeus had always made disinterest in peasant life his policy.

As he stood there for a moment, he saw someone running in the distance. As the runner closed the distance, Zacchaeus realized it was Akim. He waited on the street outside his home until Akim, sweaty and out of breath from the sprint, came to a stop in front of him.

"What's going on, Akim? Why are you running? And what's everyone talking about?" Zacchaeus asked him.

Akim, breathing hard and mopping his brow, said, "We've received news this morning about that traveling preacher—he's headed our way. Not sure when he'll arrive, but it should be in the next day or two."

Zacchaeus snorted. "Is that all? I can understand why all the peasants are stirred up about it, but I'm surprised at you, Akim.

Why are you so excited?"

"Haven't you heard, cousin?"

"Heard what?"

"About the blind man. You know the one. He sits in the dirt a few miles outside of town. You know, Asher bar Hebel, that friend of Bartimaeus. We see him sitting there every time we leave Jericho or come back," Akim answered him.

"Well, of course I know him, Akim. Known him since we were boys. What about him? Has something happened to him?" Zacchaeus asked. "It would serve him right if it did—he never has the correct tax, can't make a living, and he just sits there preying on passersby. He even asks *me* for money whenever we pass, and *he's* the one in debt to *me*!" he added haughtily.

Akim waved Zacchaeus to silence, ignoring his diatribe.

"I should say something has happened to him, cousin! He's not blind anymore."

"What's that you say? How can that be?" Zacchaeus was truly shocked at this news.

"It was this Jesus who healed them, according to witnesses. Jesus was just walking by, and they called out to him, and the preacher waved his hand or something, and now Asher can see! At least, that's what I was told—I didn't see it for myself," Akim added hastily.

"What nonsense! I swear you're the most gullible person in all of Israel. Healed a man who's been blind since birth by waving his hand—it's just not possible!"

"Well, I'm just repeating what everyone's saying, Zacchaeus. You don't have to get angry at me. They say Bartimaeus went to Galilee to see his parents."

"By everyone, I suppose you mean the ignorant peasants we have to deal with every day—those who can't pay their taxes, are always asking for more time, and who can't seem to get jobs and take care of themselves. Those people?" Zacchaeus asked with a sweep of his hand that included the entire town of Jericho.

"I guess so—but everyone's saying the same thing, Zacchaeus. They're all telling the same story," Akim said.

"You mean they're all telling the same lies!"

Akim looked crestfallen. Zacchaeus grasped him by the arm and shook it.

"Akim, Akim, how many times do I have to tell you that peasants always look for a savior, someone who will make their miserable lives better?" Zacchaeus asked him gently. "Don't believe it, cousin."

"Okay, I guess," Akim said unconvincingly. Zacchaeus gazed at him for a moment and came to a decision.

"All right," Zacchaeus declared briskly, "this is what we'll do. We'll go see Asher for ourselves. Will that help?"

"Oh yes—let's do! We'll see if what they're saying is true or not," Akim said enthusiastically.

"All right then. Let's go," Zacchaeus said, taking Akim's arm and turning his steps toward the outskirts of the town.

As they walked, they heard people talking excitedly among themselves and gesturing wildly in the direction Akim and Zacchaeus were walking. Akim was clearly trying to hear what the people were saying, cocking his head in first one direction and then another.

Zacchaeus watched him, shaking his head sadly. He'd promised to take care of Akim, and today he would. He would make sure his naive cousin was not duped by another false messiah and his promises.

He wondered though, in that secret place in his mind—where he kept his tree—*if there truly was a messiah who could heal a blind man like that, what else might he be able to do?* But he quickly dispelled such an idea. *There is no messiah. It's a creation of the blind and weak minded. And I am certainly neither.*

***

Zacchaeus and Akim came to the place where the blind beggar, Asher bar Hebel, usually sat collecting coins from generous passersby. He wasn't there. Zacchaeus looked back the way they'd come, thinking perhaps they'd passed him without knowing, but he saw nothing. The road was empty going both ways.

Zacchaeus thought it odd that Asher wasn't where he'd always been. It gave him an unsettled feeling. *Where is he? Why isn't he here, sitting in the dirt of his useless life, like he's done every day since we were children?*

"Well, Akim, it looks like we made this trek for nothing," Zacchaeus said.

Clearly disappointed, Akim asked, "What should we do?"

"Go back to town, I guess. Maybe we should call at that shack where he lives—what do you say?" Zacchaeus asked. He really wanted to prove to Akim that he, Zacchaeus, was right. He'd always been right and therefore would always take care of Akim.

"Oh, that's a great idea. Let's go!" Akim said.

So they retraced their steps back down the dusty road to Jericho, and as they came near to the outskirts about thirty minutes later, they saw a crowd gathered. They halted at the edge. Zacchaeus could not see over the heads of the people, frustrating him to no end.

"Akim, what do you see?" he asked, irritated, jumping up and down trying to get a glimpse.

"There's a man in the center, and everyone's trying to touch him, but I can't see his face," Akim replied.

"Well, can you push through so we can get closer to him?" Zacchaeus said.

"I can try," Akim said, laying his hands on the two directly in front of him. They didn't budge, even when Akim yelled at them.

Zacchaeus took over. "Here, you people, make way. Make way!" he shouted in full voice. For his short stature, he'd always had a commanding voice. The people slowly parted. Zacchaeus and Akim stepped closer to the man in the center, who now turned to face them.

"Zacchaeus, Akim!" the man said joyfully. "It's so good to

see you!"

Zacchaeus was speechless with shock. Standing before them was Asher bar Hebel. Zacchaeus couldn't think of anything to say. He hadn't recognized Asher immediately; he only knew it was him when he spoke. His face looked different somehow, but Zacchaeus couldn't put his finger on the why of it.

"Zacchaeus, it's me. Don't you recognize me?" Asher asked.

"But...but..." Zacchaeus began, but his voice failed completely.

Akim interrupted him. "But, Asher, how did you know it was us? You've never seen our faces before!" Akim asked incredulously.

"I've heard your voices for years, Akim," Asher explained. He looked at Zacchaeus. "I'd know that powerful voice anywhere, my friend."

Asher then went into a parody. "Asher bar Hebel, that's not nearly enough tax! Pay me what you owe, or I'll see you in prison today!" Asher parroted over the throng. The crowd loved it, laughing uproariously.

Zacchaeus, purple faced, veins standing out on his forehead, was not amused at all.

How dare you, you leech! I'll make you pay for this – I swear I will, he thought. He glared at Akim.

Unwanted, his tree beckoned in his mind, drawing him to the safety of its branches and leaves. He pushed the notion aside and stepped to within inches of Asher.

Asher, red faced and clearly embarrassed, waved the onlookers to silence.

"Zacchaeus, I'm sorry. I shouldn't have done that. Will you forgive me?" he asked gently, touching Zacchaeus on the shoulder.

Zacchaeus shook him off angrily.

"I won't have any of your false humility, Asher. Now, explain to us immediately what has happened to you. Why can you see us? Have you been playing us for fools all these years, pretending to be blind to gain our sympathy – and my money?"

Asher looked at Zacchaeus sadly.

"Of course not, Zacchaeus! I have been blind since birth—you all know that," Asher said, lifting his voice over the assembly.

The people closest to him nodded their heads, murmuring to each other. This wasn't going as Zacchaeus had predicted. He glanced quickly at Akim; his cousin looked confused.

"Your parents put you up to this! Say it! Your whole family has perpetrated this lie. They sent you out to beg as a small boy so that worthless father of yours wouldn't have to work and pay taxes. Admit it!" Even as Zacchaeus said the words, he knew it was futile. No one would buy this explanation.

"Oh, Zacchaeus," Asher said gently. "Here's what happened: I was born blind, and now I see. Jesus walked by on the road, and I called out to him, 'Jesus, Son of David, have mercy on me!' The people around me tried to shut me up, but I just shouted louder, 'Son of David, have mercy on me!'"

Zacchaeus said nothing, waiting.

"Zacchaeus, don't you want to know what happened next?"

Zacchaeus glared angrily at Asher, pulling himself up to his full height and throwing his shoulders back. Those closest to him nervously stepped back.

"Oh, why not?" he finally said. "Tell us your story, Asher, but don't expect any in this crowd to believe it, least of all me!"

Asher, clearly frustrated, continued his tale.

"Well, Jesus stopped and asked the people to help me over to him. And then he asked me, 'What do you want me to do for you?' I told him, 'Lord, I want to see!' And then he said, 'All right, receive your sight. Your faith has healed you.' That's all. After that, I could see as well as any of you!"

Zacchaeus, amazed, said the only thing that came to his mind. "You mean he didn't wave his hand over you?"

"Wave his hand? What are you talking about? And how should I know if he waved his hand over me—I was blind," Asher replied with a puzzled look.

The people around Zacchaeus chuckled. Zacchaeus, silent,

gazed at Asher, unable to process what he'd just heard.

"Asher," Akim asked hesitantly, "do you mean he actually cured you, just like that, of being blind? You can see as well as the rest of us?"

Akim's words brought Zacchaeus violently out of his mental fog. He tried to interject a reply, not wanting to hear Asher's answer, but Asher beat him to the punch.

"Better, Akim! I can see, but not just with my eyes! I can see with my eyes, yes, and that's wonderful." Asher's gaze quickly skimmed the crowd as he spoke. "Yes, that's wonderful," he continued, voice softer now, "but now I see with my soul too. Jesus opened my eyes *and* my heart, Akim. I will never be alone again," he finished, tears in his new eyes.

Zacchaeus could remain silent no longer.

"What utter nonsense! I don't believe a word of it. Come, Akim. We're going back to town."

But Akim did not move. He didn't even look at Zacchaeus. He stood there, hands hanging limply at his sides, mouth slightly open, tears raining down his cheeks.

"Asher, I want to meet him. Do you think he would see me and talk to me for a moment?"

Zacchaeus grabbed Akim's arm and shook it violently. "Akim, listen to me! This man you want to see is obviously a charlatan. People aren't blind one day and able to see the next. It's ludicrous! Now, come. We're going home."

Zacchaeus tried to drag him away by the arm, but his short stature and Akim's bulk made it difficult—Akim stood his ground, and the result was that Zacchaeus tripped over his own feet and fell to the ground.

Asher quickly bent over and extended his hand to help him up, but Zacchaeus slapped it away and stood without assistance, indignantly dusting his robes.

"Fine, Akim, fine! You just stay here with Asher and chase your false messiah! I'm going back to the real world." He turned to Asher. "I'll be back to collect what you owe. I assume you'll be getting a job soon, now that you've been 'healed'?" he said sarcastically.

Akim looked miserable, shoulders drooping at his cousin's words.

"Zacchaeus...wait...I didn't mean..." he began, but was cut off.

"Akim," Zacchaeus said grimly, "stay here if you want. I can get along without your help. I never needed you anyway—I was just keeping a promise to your parents. That's over now, since you obviously don't need me anymore." Turning, he stomped a few feet away but was stopped by Asher.

"Zacchaeus, wait!" Asher stepped to Zacchaeus, looking down into his eyes. He said softly, "Zacchaeus, there are many kinds of blindness. I've been healed of mine. Wouldn't you like to be healed of yours?"

"I'm not blind, you fool! Now leave me be and go back to your fantasies!" Zacchaeus shouted.

Asher shrugged his shoulders in defeat and turned back to Akim, putting an arm about the huge man's shoulders. As they walked away from Zacchaeus, trailed by the crowd, Zacchaeus heard Asher say, "Let's go find Jesus. We'll get him to tell you the story of the camel and the needle—you'll love it! He's the best storyteller, I tell you. And, Akim, if you follow Jesus, you'll never be alone again either."

Zacchaeus stood there, dust still clinging to his robes, and watched Akim, Asher, and the townspeople walk away from him. The thought arose in his mind, unbidden, that this was the picture of his whole life. *I'm always either running away from them or they're running away from me. Always alone, never belonging.*

Zacchaeus felt his carefully erected wall crumbling—the wall built by his own hand, to keep others out, to maintain control over his emotions, to protect his wealth and his reputation as a strict law abider. But now he wondered, again, as he stood in the heat of the afternoon. *What would it be like to be in the center of that crowd, to feel a kinship with another person, to* connect*?* He felt the urge, the need, to run after Asher and Akim, to beg to go with them. But as soon as it arose, he beat it down in his mind. *No, I don't need them. I don't need anyone.*

He shook his head and turned his steps drearily toward home. As soon as he did, he felt the comfortable, the familiar sense of control drift over him, and he knew he'd made the right decision. *Let them chase their dreams. The messiah they seek will pass away out of their sight in due time, and another will rise up. It's always the same.*

And as always, these thoughts became the glue with which the crumbling wall remade itself—stronger than ever—enclosing his tree of refuge to which Zacchaeus could always retreat, hiding himself from *them*, from his need. It was to the tree that Zacchaeus headed now, where his bag of coin rested and his self-sufficiency and pride awaited his arrival. He would linger there again, counting his money, his accomplishments, reveling in his elite position and the respect due him.

Zacchaeus hurried now, the tree, with its seductive security beckoning him on. He couldn't wait to climb its trunk and hide among its wide, leafy branches. *This time, I won't come down. This time I'll stay there. I don't need them.*

Poor Zacchaeus! I feel sorry for him, don't you? He doesn't know it, but Asher was right. There are many kinds of blindness—and the whole of humanity suffers from them all.

Zacchaeus was blinded by his wealth. The flash of gold obscured his sight, blinding him to his need.

> The love of money is a root of all kinds of evil. Some people, eager for money, have wandered from the faith and pierced themselves with many griefs.
> (1Timothy 6:10)

Zacchaeus is pierced by many griefs—hard-heartedness, a grasping, vindictive nature, his vision narrowed down by one thought: *how to get more?* And loneliness dogs him. No matter how fast he tries to run away from himself, even to the tree, when he arrives, he still faces himself. Have you found that true in your own life? I have. We can never outrun ourselves.

Love of money springs from love of self—a sin implanted in our DNA by our first parents' rebellion and for which there is only one antidote. The grace of our Lord Jesus Christ is the medicine Zacchaeus needs, just as we do.

The climax of Zacchaeus's story is just around the corner. The moment for which God has been working and waiting has arrived. Hold on to your hats as the God of the universe prepares—with all of heaven's hosts watching wide eyed—to enter Zacchaeus's life.

As Zacchaeus reached his street, he saw a commotion up ahead. A group of street ruffians stood in a circle, shouting. As he came closer, he could hear the cries of another within the circle. Dust flew as the boys kicked their feet and reached down and picked up dirt and small stones and flung them onto the ground in front of them.

Instantly, and hardly understanding himself, Zacchaeus became enraged. He charged into the middle of them, knocking two of them to the ground. As he reached the center, he saw a small boy lying there, bleeding from a cut above his eyebrow and covered with dirt. His sobs twisted like a knife into Zacchaeus's heart, shortening his breath, making his head pound. A familiar feeling of dread overtook him. He dropped to his knees next to the small boy and touched his forehead. The boy looked up at him out of twin pools of misery, wiping the back of his small hand across his bleeding nose.

"It'll be okay, boy," Zacchaeus whispered. "Just stay still."

Zacchaeus stood up and faced the gang, who now loomed in front of him. Several were snickering, looking down at him. Two on the left took a menacing step toward him.

"Walk away, little man," one sneered. "You have no business here."

Another stepped forward and shoved Zacchaeus in the chest. "Just who do you think you are, anyway? Go home before you get hurt!" He shoved Zacchaeus again, causing him to stumble over the boy on the ground.

He fell flat on his back, the little boy under him—who immediately began shrieking in pain. The mob of bullies sniggered at Zacchaeus, lying at their feet, dazed from banging his head on the hard-packed dirt.

They were closing in on him again. Zacchaeus hurriedly got to his feet and backed away. As they moved in, one brute kicked the small boy in the groin, setting off another round of howling laughter as their victim groaned in pain.

Zacchaeus had had enough. He turned and ran a few yards away, stumbling a little, still dazed by the bump on his head. He heard a commotion behind him again and stopped. Turning, he saw the tanner from across the street, a giant of a man, wade into the gang of boys and send them packing with a few well-placed punches. Then he picked up the small boy, set him on his feet, took his hand, and led him down the street, presumably to the boy's home.

Humiliation washed over Zacchaeus, bringing hot tears to his eyes. As he turned his steps once again toward home, brushing the dirt from his fine robes, smoothing his hair and beard, he saw some townspeople staring and gesturing toward him, whispering. He quickly looked away and pretended not to notice. *So what? At least I tried to help the poor little boy. It's more than they did! It's more than anyone ever did for me.* He raised a fist at them, puffing out his chest in pride, swallowing the pain he shared with the small boy.

***

The next day, Zacchaeus awoke slowly, the furious pounding in his head resolving itself into a furious pounding on his front door. He'd overslept. He shuffled to the door and found Akim on the other side.

"Oh, it's you. What do you want, Akim? I'm not dressed, and I haven't eaten," Zacchaeus said disagreeably, rubbing his forehead.

"May I come in, cousin? I came to see if there's anything I can do for you today," Akim said kindly. Zacchaeus stared for a moment, not really wanting company. Finally, he stepped aside and waved Akim in.

Akim walked through the doorway into the sitting area.

"Is your servant still away, Zacchaeus?" he asked politely.

"Yes, that worthless...yes, he's still away. He was only supposed to be gone to Alexandrium for a couple of days for the wedding, but he's not back yet—probably taking advantage of my generosity again, thinking I'll just take him back. I'm thinking about hiring someone else since he doesn't seem to want to work for a living, like so many other people in this dirty little town." Zacchaeus had been thinking no such thing, but now it sounded like a good idea. *Generosity is quite fatiguing.*

Akim grimaced and looked away.

"Well, what's eating you now, Akim? I have a perfect right to get rid of a substandard employee, don't I? I can't afford to coddle him. Either he works, or he doesn't."

"Zacchaeus, you don't have to be mean and fire him—maybe he's ill, or maybe robbers attacked him on the road."

"Right!" Zacchaeus said sarcastically. "Really, Akim, you're much too tenderhearted. He'll probably wander into town with some trumped-up story to gain my sympathy. Well, I won't be taken in by anyone, do you hear?"

Akim sighed and shook his head at his cousin. "Look, I'd be glad to help out while he's gone. Why didn't you ask me? Here," he said, picking up a bowl from the small table in the eating area, "let me tidy up for you a little. I'm sure you have important things to do."

"And I suppose you want me to pay you?" Zacchaeus said irritably.

"No, no, of course not!" Akim countered immediately. "You're my cousin, Zacchaeus. I don't need to be paid to help you out. Please, just let me help, okay?"

"Fine, then. Help out all you want, but don't expect the least payment from me—are we clear? Do I have to put it in writing?" Zacchaeus grumbled.

"Of course you don't have to put it in writing!" Akim declared. He picked up a scroll from the floor and placed it on the table. He grabbed a bowl to take to the back porch to be cleaned. When he returned, he stopped in the doorway and stared at Zacchaeus.

"What now, Akim? Why do you stare at me like that? I thought you were here to help me."

"Zacchaeus, what's eating you? I can't tell if you're angry at me, sad, or what. And why do you keep rubbing the back of your head?" Akim asked kindly.

Zacchaeus unleashed on Akim.

"Why are you being so nice to me, Akim? Do you want something from me? Just say it then! What do you want?" Zacchaeus shouted, waving his arms.

Akim hastily stepped back.

"I…I…no, cousin, you've got it all wrong! I didn't come here to ask you for anything. I just came here to help you. I realized yesterday that I only help you when you pay me. I now think that's wrong. We're family. We're basically all we've got, and I should be willing to help you when you need it. You've taken care of me practically all my life, and all I do for you is work for payment. It shouldn't be that way between us," Akim finished, wringing his hands in his passion.

Zacchaeus stared, speechless for a moment. He'd never heard anything like that from Akim before, or anyone else for that matter. He didn't know what to do with it. No one had ever wanted to help him without expecting something in return. It was the world in which he lived, the world he'd created for himself—business, all business. And he himself had never done anything for others without expecting a return. Finally,

Zacchaeus found his voice.

"What's happened to you, Akim?" he asked curiously. "Did you fall down and hit your head or something? Has a spirit possessed you, causing you to say these things to me?"

Akim shook his head vigorously, smiling broadly. "I'm glad you asked! I met Jesus. Just that. He's changed my life—I'm not alone anymore!"

"Ah," Zacchaeus said with a condescending look. "And did he wave his hand over you and 'heal' you, as he did Asher bar Hebel?"

Akim's shoulders drooped at the sneering tone. Zacchaeus waited for Akim to give up and agree with his logical view of things—just as he had always done since they were children—but it didn't happen.

"No, Zacchaeus. He changed my heart, someplace where you can't see. I'm a different person than I was yesterday."

The firmness of Akim's voice was different. Zacchaeus couldn't respond, because Akim *was* different than yesterday.

"Zacchaeus, Jesus is God! He really is—I believe that now with all my heart. He explained everything to me yesterday. I didn't understand all of it, but this is what I do understand: he is God, and he will rule us someday, without Rome, without the corrupt priests."

"Blasphemy!" Zacchaeus declared, his eyes locked on Akim's. But his answer had no effect.

"No, cousin. Not blasphemy. Truth," Akim said gently, with a new authority. "Zacchaeus, I want you to meet him."

"I don't need him," Zacchaeus said weakly, trying to gain control of this disturbing conversation. "I don't need anyone, Akim," he finished in a whisper.

"Oh, Zacchaeus, that's where you're wrong. Jesus told me yesterday that it's when I think I don't need anyone that I really do. But not just anyone—I need him! And so do you, cousin," Akim said softly, tenderly, compassion shining out of his eyes.

Zacchaeus stared at the face he'd known since Akim was a baby—himself not much older—and had to admit there was something different. The worry lines were gone, the avarice and self-seeking were gone. Where there was hardness, particularly around the eyes, there was a new softness. *It's as if a mask has dropped from Akim's face, revealing a person unknown to me.*

An unfamiliar feeling of guilt stabbed Zacchaeus, for it came to him suddenly that he, Zacchaeus, was responsible for Akim's covetousness, his lack of conscience. He had raised Akim when his parents died, carefully crafting him in his own image, to make of him the perfect tax-farming assistant—for himself, always for himself. But now Akim had met someone else who had unmade all of that in the space of a few hours, and Akim now begged him to come and meet his new friend. *Well, that's just not going to happen!*

"I think you should leave, Akim. I have no interest in your blasphemy or your false messiah, just as I no longer have interest in you," Zacchaeus said unemotionally, turning away.

"Zacchaeus, please, I didn't mean to offend…" Akim started, clearly crushed.

Without turning around, Zacchaeus waved his cousin away, saying brutally, "Akim, get out of my presence! I won't have you in my home anymore, nor in my employ!" Zacchaeus turned, face suffused in purple. "Get out!" It didn't move him at all that his younger cousin stood there, tears streaming down his face, and then fell to his knees in front of him.

"Zacchaeus, cousin, please forgive my offense—please!" Akim begged.

"Fine, I forgive you," he said. "Now leave. I've got work to do." His tone was harsh and unyielding. He looked not at Akim but over his head.

Finally, Akim moved to the door, opened it, and hesitated. He started to say something, but Zacchaeus turned his back on him and shuffled through a pile of scrolls. After a few moments, Zacchaeus heard the door close softly.

He dropped the scrolls and sat down heavily in a nearby chair, head in his hands. *What have I done? No! He did it, that weak minded cousin of mine! This was not my doing – he brought it on himself. Jesus...God! What nonsense, what utter nonsense!*

Zacchaeus sat there for some time, his thoughts first accusing and then excusing himself. They flew round and round in his head, and whichever way they stopped, he saw Akim kneeling in front of him, begging his forgiveness, pleading with him to meet Jesus. His aching head and his aching, lonely heart threatened to destroy him.

Finally, he fell asleep there, sagging into the chair, curled up with his feet tucked under him, trying to make the chair a cocoon in which he could hide. As his burning eyes closed, he dreamed and saw the child – the boy at his feet, beaten and bloody. The taunting of the bullies sounded just behind him. Compassion and anger welled up in him once more. In his dream, he slowly reached out his hand to turn the boy over.

Zacchaeus groaned in his sleep, for as he rolled the boy over, it was his own face he saw. His eyes snapped open, and he was alone. Zacchaeus crumpled even smaller in the chair and sobbed, pain racking his head and his chest.

What have I done?

What have I done? I lay on my bed, hiding in my tree, weeping tears of grief and self-loathing. I'd locked my mother out of my life. Just like Zacchaeus with Akim, I'd cut her off, preferring to dwell on her failures and affronts than to forgive her frailties and spiritual handicaps.

For five years or so, we hardly spoke to each other, as I hardened my heart against the woman who'd given me life, cared for me, worked hard for her family, and tenderly let me leave the nest when I was eighteen.

Years later, in woeful, Zacchaeus-like pride and arrogance, I turned away from her when she needed me most. She was locked in emotional pain that I—her daughter, judge, and jury—decided was her own fault, and so there was no need for me to be part of it or to offer comfort.

I was angry at decisions she'd made that hurt me and the rest of the family. That anger clouded our relationship until the day I watched her die. I wanted God to punish her. I thought, after we began speaking again, that it was up to me to point out her transgressions, remind her over and over again what bitterness could do to a person if not unchecked. But for every word I spoke to her in anger, a brick of bitterness was laid in my own heart, building an impenetrable wall between us.

Sadly, unknown to me during this time—really, for many years before—dementia was taking hold in Mom's brain. It crept in so slowly that Dad, my brother, and I had no idea what was happening. We didn't understand the change in her, that her behavior over those many years could have its seeds in the disease ravaging her. By the time I realized what was taking place inside her, it was too late to even apologize and to make amends in a way she would understand. Because of the dementia, she was stuck in her bitterness, locked inside a prison with no escape to repentance.

But I suffered from a more severe and devastating form of the disease—spiritual dementia. I had forgotten the many sins of which I'd been forgiven, and so could not forgive her.

I wept, for I knew that God would not judge her—He would judge *me* for the arrogance that led me to sever a relationship. As I lay there, making my confession to God for my own bitterness, I knew I must let it go. There was nothing Mom could do about what she'd done, but there was everything I could do about what I'd done.

Zacchaeus awoke stiff and uncomfortable from spending the night in the chair instead of his own bed. He berated himself for such nonsense. *Why do I let such things as this false messiah and Akim's wild claims upset me so? It means nothing to me.* He determined now to do two things: clean up the mess in his house and get to work on his accounts. They were in disarray, and there would be a reckoning with Rome if he did not straighten it out without delay.

He felt better just making this plan. Soon, he had his small home clean and orderly. Then he sat at his table, his scrolls in front of him, busily adding up his recent collections. The neat columns with their totals, larger than he thought, soothed him. This was his world, the world in which he felt comfortable, where everything made sense, the world where everything was predictable, where he was in charge. The neat columns always added up correctly, and when balanced, he felt a sense of calm—here in this world, the familiar world, there was no chaos, no turmoil.

He worked contentedly for a few hours until he felt hungry. He set aside his work and went to his cupboard for bread. As he did, he heard a commotion out in the street. He stepped to the window and peered out. His neighbors, many of them, all ran in the same direction, shouting something he couldn't make out and pointed to the road which lead out of Jericho. He couldn't tell if it was some joy or disaster they yelled about.

He opened his front door and stepped out to his small porch. He heard clearly the word *Jesus!* shouted by the small child who lived next to him. He turned to look at the child, his small shoulders held securely by his mother. She looked at him and spoke hastily.

"Oh, sir, we are sorry to disturb your peace. Please forgive our excitement, but Jesus of Nazareth is coming, and we want to see him," the woman said.

Zacchaeus stared at her, the thought circling in his mind, *Again? Not again. Must I deal with this fantasy again?* But his curiosity got the best of him.

"Tell me," he finally asked her, "why do you want to see him?"

She picked up her child and walked closer to where Zacchaeus stood on his porch.

"Because he is my king, sir," she said simply.

"That's treason, woman!" Zacchaeus accused.

"Well, if you say so, sir. But I'd rather claim him as my king than go on as I was before. After my husband—you know he died last year—after he was gone, the loneliness almost killed me. But I'm not alone anymore," she joyfully declared. "And for that, I'd gladly face a traitor's death. Jesus has filled my heart, and I know he is my king and will be forever."

King?

Zacchaeus, astonished, said nothing.

She put her son down, took his hand, and turned toward the street. He watched as they slowly walked in the direction everyone else was going, the boy hopping erratically about, until he couldn't see them anymore. He felt an unfamiliar shame that, no, he didn't know her husband had died last year. He never paid attention to the personal problems of those around him—unless they didn't pay their taxes—and then he was subjected to their tales of woe.

On the heels of that unfamiliar feeling was another. As he watched them turn the corner, surrounded by other townspeople going the same direction, talking and laughing together, that loneliness of which she'd spoken swamped him without warning, threatening to drown him. He stepped slowly off the porch and sat down heavily on the old stump outside his home, arms hanging limply, face blank.

I'm lonely. I have no one who cares for me. I am alone in the world, surrounded by my gold and my scrolls.

The dream arose, once again, of the little boy in the street, pummeled black and blue by vicious, uncaring bullies, his own face in place of the little boy's face. But now the vision had changed. Instead of seeing his own face on the little boy, he now saw it as each of the street ruffians turned and glared at him, daring him to interfere—and he knew. I'm *the bully now.* I'm *the one beating people black and blue.* I'm *the one chasing the innocents down the street, demanding their livelihoods.*

It was too much. Zacchaeus was driven to his knees, there in his yard, by the inescapable conclusion that he was not a righteous man—he was just as much a poor sinner as all those around him. He sobbed at the thought. He thought to run for his tree, but for the first time in his life, his tree wasn't large enough, safe enough. As he desperately sought it, tried to climb it in his mind, the branches kept breaking under his weight—the weight of his guilt and shame.

He got to his feet and began walking down the street. *I must find this Jesus. I must see if he's a charlatan for myself. If he is, well, I'll be proved right. If he isn't...* Zacchaeus didn't know how to finish the thought.

What Zacchaeus doesn't know, of course, is that *he* is not choosing this path—the path to Jesus, whom he suspects of being a flimflam. God had wooed him all his life, gradually shrinking his tree of refuge, drawing him with cords of love to see for himself who Jesus is. And he's finally beginning the journey—with God watching every step, waiting in delighted anticipation for the meeting to take place.

Zacchaeus came to the corner everyone else had rounded, and stopped. No one was there. He looked to his right toward a poorer section of Jericho and saw in the distance a large group of townspeople. He walked quickly toward them, now realizing they were close to his childhood home. He could even see his boyhood tree, older now, leaves thinning, branches broken off and lying on the ground, but it still stood strong and sturdy. He felt comforted looking at it.

He stood on the fringes, unable to see what everyone was

looking at.

"What's going on?" he asked a man standing nearby.

The man looked at him and turned away. "What's it to you, *Mr.* Zacchaeus?" He snorted.

With an effort, Zacchaeus quelled his pride-driven anger.

"I'm just curious," he said humbly, looking up at the man who towered above him.

"Well, if you must know, we're waiting for Jesus of Nazareth to arrive. It's said he's almost here with his disciples. He was in the area yesterday, and now he's on his way back." The man broke off as the people in front of the throng began yelling.

"There he is!"

"He's coming!"

"He's here! He's here!"

The crowd surged forward, clearly united in their need to be close to Jesus.

Zacchaeus could not break through the crowd to see. He pushed and pulled at people, but they would not move out of his way. He felt desperate, like a dying man in the desert, stretching with all his strength for a cup of cold water just out of reach.

He looked to his right and saw his tree again. He looked back at the bodies and heads in front of him. He could hear people in the front talking, laughing, and crying "Jesus!" And he could hear the soft responses from the man he couldn't see.

Making a sudden decision, he sprinted for his tree and swarmed up the trunk as if twelve years old again. He crept out onto the biggest limb, now hanging a little lower than when he was a boy. Pushing the straggly leaves aside, he finally got his first look at Jesus of Nazareth.

Humph! He looks like just another peasant.

Jesus leaned over and patted the head of a child, the child who lived next door to Zacchaeus. The enraptured looks on the faces of the boy and his mother were a wonder to Zacchaeus. *What could produce that kind of joy?*

Then Jesus took the hands of an elderly woman and danced

a little jig with her, making her giggle. As he twirled her around, he leaned over and whispered something that made her face light up even more, smoothing the wrinkles, causing her to look years younger. Then he kissed her gently on the cheek.

The joy of the people was palpable.

They're connected to Jesus in some way.

As Zacchaeus watched, Jesus touched one after another, speaking soft words. He was impeded in his progress by women kneeling before him, kissing his feet, clasping his legs. Zacchaeus recognized, for the first time in his life, *community*. And for the first time, as Jesus approached his tree and stopped directly under it, Zacchaeus truly wanted what these people had. Tears sprang to his eyes as he realized he saw before him something he'd never experienced—friendship, love, and connection with no strings attached.

As the throng stopped with Jesus, Zacchaeus saw Akim in the center of the mass, arms locked with Levi—the tax-collector-turned-Jesus-follower—in close conversation.

Maybe they're talking about me. Maybe Akim is telling Levi what a rotten scoundrel I am. Maybe... Zacchaeus couldn't finish his thought because Jesus suddenly spoke loudly—he'd stepped under the branch to which Zacchaeus clung and looked directly at him.

"Zacchaeus! Quick, come down! I must be a guest in your home today."

The crowd stilled.

Zacchaeus, startled, almost fell from his perch. He heard delighted laughter, Jesus among them, as he desperately tried to hang on and finally righted himself. For a moment, Zacchaeus's well-ordered world turned upside down. Blazing light replaced the darkness in his heart, for with those simple, everyday words spoken by Jesus, Zacchaeus knew with certainty he'd encountered God. Explanation would defy him in the days to come—he couldn't have told anyone why he knew—he just knew. And with the knowing came an intense longing, such as he'd never experienced, to know more.

He climbed down and walked slowly to Jesus. This time the people graciously parted for him. He felt pats on his back as he walked among them, heard kind murmurings of encouragement as he now stood toe to toe with Jesus.

The mob quieted as Zacchaeus looked up into the face of Jesus and then immediately slipped to his knees.

King? Yes! God? Yes!

Head bowed, hands trembling, he worshiped.

He felt a warm hand on his head and heard a soft whisper in his ear. "Your name is Zacchaeus—*purity*. Now you will live up to your name, my son."

Looking up, he was astonished to see Jesus kneeling in front of him. Jesus cupped his large, calloused hands around Zacchaeus's face.

"Zacchaeus, you have much in this world. But I come to unmake all of that and give you much in the world to come. Will you follow me?"

Zacchaeus didn't even have to think about it. The longing in his heart had grown until it was bursting and now came rushing out of his mouth like water from a burst dam.

"Yes, Jesus, I will follow you," he said. The crowd erupted around him at those words, joyful exclamations, clapping, and laughter ringing out over the town.

"Excellent, my friend, excellent!" Jesus exclaimed. He extended his hand to help Zacchaeus up.

No one's ever called me that unless they wanted something from me. And have I ever called anyone that unless I wanted something? Zacchaeus shook his head in wonder.

He gazed around at the townspeople, momentarily stopped on Levi, and had a sudden inspiration.

"My Lord, I will follow you—but you must now follow *me*, to my home for a party," he said, and then added in his biggest voice, "and you're all invited!"

The crowd erupted in joyful applause.

Several, however, stood on the fringes, looking unhappy.

They pointed their fingers at Zacchaeus as he walked next to Jesus. Zacchaeus could hear their grumbling words.

"Jesus is going to the home of a tax collector!"

"How dare he—consorting with the enemy!"

"He defiles himself! How can he be who he says he is?"

And two men, priests, walked away, deep in conversation, looking back at Jesus furtively as they talked. Zacchaeus watched them go, wondering what they were saying about *him*.

Zacchaeus suddenly didn't care what anyone thought of him. He turned back to Jesus and said, "You are welcome in my home, Jesus. Come. I'll show you where I live."

Jesus laughed delightedly and said, "My friend, I already know where you live! I've been there before. I've watched you, stood next to you as you pored over your scrolls, counting your gold to the last shekel, and I've longed to give you real gold." Jesus paused and placed his hand on the gnarled wood of the old tree, stroking it lovingly.

"I created this tree for you, Zacchaeus, and I've climbed it with you all your life as you sought refuge from those bullies. And I was there when you tried to hide among its leaves from your own sin."

He smiled broadly at Zacchaeus. "I don't think you'll be needing this tree anymore, nor the one up here, my friend," he said, gently tapping Zacchaeus's forehead. "Do you?"

"No, I don't think I'll be climbing trees anymore, Jesus, now that I've got you!" With a grin, he added, "I'm getting too old for that anyway!"

Jesus laughed again, and putting his arm around Zacchaeus, they walked back into Jericho, talking softly, followed by Zacchaeus's new friends.

***

They arrived at Zacchaeus's home. Some of the disciples sent the townspeople away to bring food from their own homes to make a feast. Zacchaeus provided from his cupboards, ably assisted by Akim, who couldn't stop smiling. Children shrieked and played outside, watched over by their relatives.

Zacchaeus and Akim worked together in companionable silence, preparing vegetables, bread, and cheese—Zacchaeus had sent Akim to the market earlier for supplies—until Zacchaeus couldn't stand it anymore. He put his knife down and turned to face Akim.

"Akim, please forgive me for the way I treated you, have always treated you," he said, tears spilling down his face.

"Zacchaeus, cousin," Akim began, choking on his words, "I forgave you the moment I met Jesus and was forgiven of my own sins toward you and others. Jesus says we can't experience forgiveness fully until we forgive all those who have trespassed against us. But I thank you for asking—you don't know how much that means to me. To see the change in you today is the most wonderful thing I've ever experienced, except for my own salvation."

"Thank you, my friend," Zacchaeus replied in a husky voice. He looked at Akim and had a curious thought. *Akim doesn't seem now to be so much taller than me! Maybe it's because I'm not such a little man anymore since I met Jesus.*

Later, as the people were feasting joyously, Zacchaeus suddenly stood up in the midst of them.

"People, *my…my friends,*" he said, stumbling over the unfamiliar phrase, "my friends, I have something to say." His guests quieted as Zacchaeus made his way through those sitting on the floor to a hidden cupboard in the wall. He opened the small hinged door and slowly reached in, drawing out the moment.

He took something out of the cupboard and turned to face his guests, quickly shifting whatever it was behind his back. He gazed at the faces of these, his *friends,* heart swelling in gratitude to the one whose eyes now pierced his own. Zacchaeus held Jesus's eyes for a moment, saw him nod slightly, knowingly.

With a dramatic flourish, Zacchaeus whipped the heavy leather bag from behind him and held it up so all could see it.

Looking straight at Jesus, Zacchaeus announced loudly, "Today, I promise to give half my wealth to the poor."

Those before him, and those crowded through the windows and doors and standing outside in the yard, erupted in joyful applause.

"But that's not all, my friends! I have cheated you, year after miserable year. I have charged you more than Rome required of me, and I kept the overage for myself. I confess that to you now."

The crowd quieted at those words, looking with sad eyes at the broken man in front of them. Zacchaeus felt the hot tears rising behind his eyelids, but he didn't care anymore about his image. All he cared about was pleasing his King. He struggled to regain control of his voice, tears sliding down his face.

"I promise you I will make restitution to all those I have cheated. Beginning tomorrow, I will go through my accounts in detail and determine exactly how much I have collected over and above what I was supposed to, and I will pay back four times as much—to all of you."

His guests sat in shocked silence. The notorious tax collector, the pompous blowhard, the man who'd had many of them and their relatives thrown into prison until they paid their taxes, now stood before them humbled and contrite.

Into the silence Jesus of Nazareth spoke.

"Salvation has come to this home today, for this man has shown himself to be a true son of Abraham." Jesus arose from his place on the floor—where several children had vied for his lap—and threaded his way through the people, arriving at the side of Zacchaeus. He grabbed Zacchaeus in a bear hug, long and tight.

Then, turning to the people, he said, "For the Son of Man came to seek and save those who are lost." He looked into Zacchaeus's eyes and added, "My son, you are now found. And I will never leave you nor forsake you."

The room erupted again. And out in the yard, joyous applause, cries of exultation, and praises to God would continue long into the night. The party was in full swing.

At that moment, in his mind's eye, Zacchaeus saw his tree lying in pieces on the ground as if toppled by a strong wind. Then the strong wind blew it away as if it had never existed.

Zacchaeus, hours later, looked around his small home crowded with his noisy neighbors, children jumping around, shrieking in laughter, dropping crumbs everywhere in his living space—and thought he'd never seen such a beautiful sight. *Jericho has never seen such a celebration as this.*

His eyes met those of Jesus across the room, the unspoken thought clear between them.

The transformation is complete.

And in the heavens, another party was in full swing as the angels celebrated another homecoming of a lost soul to Creator God, who never slumbers or sleeps and who is relentless in His passionate pursuit of relationship with His creations.

From hated tax collector to beloved friend and neighbor; from a small man who used his wealth and position to be a big man; from an abused childhood—becoming an abuser himself—to a generous, giving man who now knew his wealth was useless to gain true happiness, Zacchaeus had been transformed by Jesus of Nazareth.

Pride and arrogance led Zacchaeus down the road of loneliness and isolation. Money was his god, power and influence his ambitions, and he found it all filthy rags when he met Jesus. God so pursued him, ran him down, enveloping him, until he was brought to the end of himself and to the realization that nothing counts in this world except *relationship*—with God and with others. Zacchaeus chose salvation over destruction.

In Randy Alcorn's *Grace – a Bigger View of God's Love* (Harvest House Publishers, July 2016, p. 144) he says, "The only way to survive prosperity is, by God's grace, to view money and possessions as gifts from his gracious hand and to use them generously to help others."

And from the same page, a quote from Andrew Murray—"The world asks, 'What does a man own?' Christ asks, 'How does he use it?'" And so many centuries after Zacchaeus's encounter with God, we still learn the same lessons.

My own journey from pride and arrogance took a different path, and I'm still walking away from it, with my hand in the Master's hand. I've never cared much about having money and stuff, but that didn't let me off the hook.

I was always a proud little thing, even when I was very young. I can blame it on being a middle child or the oldest girl, but even so, God calls it sin. I thought I was better than my brothers and my sister, smarter, more responsible, and if our parents praised me for anything, it went right to my head and lodged there. And I am short, like Zacchaeus, so I know what it's like to always look up at people. When I was a teenager, I would have given anything for three or four more inches.

God started chipping away at my inflated ego as soon as I became a believer in the Lord Jesus Christ. It hurt—a lot sometimes—but He is so loving, He couldn't bear to leave me the way I was. And He still lovingly, and with great patience, reminds me who He is and who I am.

The breadth and depth of my pride was driven home when Mom came to live with my husband and me. Throughout that year and a half, I struggled mightily *against* relinquishing my ideas of what she needed to do to repent of her rebellion. But as they say in the *Star Trek* land of the Borg, *resistance is futile*. God was intently working on *me*, not her! And so began the hard work of letting go of the past in favor of living in the present. God forgives past tragedies, but as we practice forgiveness, He reshapes us in the *present* to look more like Him.

And then came the day when I, with my brother at my side, said goodbye to her. God allowed us the blessing of being with her for several days before she died. The night before she went to be with Jesus, I slept next to her with my hand on her chest as she lay unconscious. It was the last thing I could do for her.

I dozed next to her, waking when caregivers came in to check on us, while my brother slept fitfully in the recliner next to us.

Many times throughout that long night, feeling the gentle rise and fall of her chest under my hand, I remembered how many nights she had comforted me in my childhood—cleaned my skinned knees, wiped the tears from face, and spoke words of encouragement when I suffered the tough emotions of a teenage girl. She was always there for me.

And I remembered, with God's gentle prodding, that I hadn't always been there for her. When she'd needed me most, I turned away from her because she hadn't lived up to *my* standard. At that gentle prodding, I wanted to run for *my* tree of refuge, to escape from the pain, but God in His mercy took my hand and gently drew me to Himself as I repented of my pride. He drew me to the only Tree of refuge there is—the cross of Jesus Christ. And so, as my dear mother journeyed home, I left all my rebellion there at the foot of His tree.

I'd like to say that I've finally given up all my pride and arrogance, but I can't. I still find shards of it every day. I kick them out of my way, confessing them, and move back into God's grace, sheltering there in the shadow of the cross.

Zacchaeus's tree of refuge was the place to which he ran when he was abused as a young boy, the place in his mind to which he ran as an adult to escape his self-made loneliness, the place that always welcomed him without making him accountable. His pride was soothed there, the leaves hiding him from his own pain and the pain he created in the lives of others.

When he met Jesus, he found the Tree of refuge that would shower him with grace while washing away the pride, arrogance, and pain that had shaped his life. Zacchaeus chose *that* Tree and turned his back forever on the other.

Dear reader, what is your tree of refuge, and from what do you hide?

Loneliness?

Fear of the future?

Old age?

The piled-up sins of your youth, unconfessed and crowding your mind?

Zacchaeus calls you to come down and meet Jesus, your only Tree of refuge.

Jesus, be my Tree of refuge today.

Study Questions—The Tree

1. How did Zacchaeus's childhood experiences contribute to the man he became?
2. At what point in our lives must we stop blaming our childhood experiences for who we are today? How can we acknowledge the truth that we are shaped by those experiences without excusing ourselves?
3. What emotions were evoked in you as Zacchaeus saw his own face on the child he tried to rescue from the town bullies?
4. Describe, in your own words, how God used Zacchaeus's past to draw him to Himself, the only real refuge for Zacchaeus.
5. From what do you need refuge today? Are you hiding in your self-made tree—or in the lap of your Creator, who made you and knows exactly what you need?

Chapter 6
Pardoned

But the mob shouted louder and louder, demanding that Jesus be crucified, and their voices prevailed. So Pilate sentenced Jesus to die as they demanded. As they had requested, he released Barabbas, the man in prison for insurrection and murder. But he turned Jesus over to them to do as they wished.

—Luke 23:23–25

Searching the mass of humanity in front of him, he spied his target. Swiftly making his way to the man's side, he lightly touched his arm. Surprised, the man turned. Not recognizing him, his target tried to back away.

He gripped his victim's arm tightly as he drew the *sica* out of the folds of his cloak. As the surprised man struggled, the attacker drove the dagger home, feeling the long blade penetrate under the victim's breastbone. Holding him upright for a moment, he brought the dead man's face close to his lips and pretended to whisper something, giving him time to withdraw the dripping weapon and hide it in his cloak again. Then rummaging quickly through the man's garment while still supporting him, he found the heavy leather bag. Quickly, he secreted it into his own clothing.

The crowd flowed around them as he let the man sink slowly to the ground, tearing a small piece of the man's garment as he settled. The man in the cloak then turned and strolled leisurely away, losing himself in the mob of passersby. It wasn't until he was in the next street that he heard the outcry raised. Their voices faded away as Barabbas hurried in the opposite direction. He must make his report to his friends, Jewish patriots who had given themselves to the overthrow of Rome and her priestly cohorts.

He chuckled to himself as he made his way through the crowded streets. *One more enemy of the people dispatched, never to lay another law or burden on the backs of the commoner, never again to betray good patriots.* He judged it a good day's work, and he was ready to go home to his family for a few days' needed rest before his next assignment.

Jerusalem in the years leading up to the crucifixion of Jesus Christ, and in the several decades after, culminating in the fall of the city in AD 70, was not a place for the faint of heart.

Twenty centuries later, the world is not much different. The underlying political and cultural reasons for the chaotic conditions were different, but the results are the same—the brutal deaths of many innocent people and the clamping down of a despotic government on the masses. Rome—finally taking control of all previous ruling factions—surely adhered to the maxim "Don't waste a good crisis," one still followed by governments today, even in "thc land of the free and the home of the brave."

Unrest was rampant. Roman rule of Palestine was tyrannical and brutal. Jewish zealot groups sprang up, most just as brutal as their Roman conquerors. These zealots were determined to be ruled by no one. Murders were a dime a dozen, reminding us of Chicago, Washington DC, New York, and many other areas in the world today.

One such shadowy group of Jewish radicals, called Sicarii, operated during these times, coming to the fore after the fall of Jerusalem. These were assassins who carried long daggers called *sicae* and who murdered people—people whom the Sicarii determined were a threat to Jewish religious and political freedom—in broad daylight. In Acts 21:38, they were called "dagger men." The apostle Paul was accused by the Jerusalem authorities of being part of this group when a riot broke out after he'd preached.

Barabbas may have been part of a precursor to this group. The Scriptures call him a murderer and an insurrectionist. Ironically, Jesus was also accused of insurrection.

But God, in His infinite wisdom and mercy, has chosen Barabbas—*son of a father*—for a pivotal part in the great unfolding drama of redemption. He, of course, doesn't realize that, and as evidenced by his lifestyle, probably wasn't interested in knowing that. But God *will* have His way with those He chooses. Barabbas will have a front-row seat as the Master of the universe steps down from His seat of judgment and becomes the judged, changing places with the guilty.

Barabbas will find himself nose to nose with his Creator, on the cusp of the most important event in the history of humanity. And with that, the most important decision of his life: choose the eternal, or stick with the temporal.

Barabbas thought it was time to go home. He had met with the others in their cave hideout in the Judean hills near Jerusalem, confirmed his success by displaying the bloody blade and piece of torn cloth, turned over the bag of gold, and received his payment and his congratulations.

As he made his way through the crowded streets, he realized he hadn't seen his wife and daughters for four days and nights. He missed them. It was for them that he'd become what he was, for them that he hid in dark corners in the night, watching, always watching for an opportunity to rid the earth of the enemies of his people. He'd spent the last four days stalking the man he'd just dispatched, learning his habits, who his friends were, where he lived and frequented. It wasn't hard. The man was full of himself, his focus on the ladder he climbed to impress Rome. Barabbas knew for a fact that the man, Eldad—*beloved of God*—had been responsible for the crucifixion and burning of at least two patriots, and probably more. *Well, now "beloved of God" was with his god in the realm of the dead, and good riddance to him!*

Changing course, he turned down a small side street in the Lower City and headed east, toward the Water Gate. Now he hurried, wanting to slip into his home with as little fanfare as possible. He could visualize his beloved wife, Adina, and their two beautiful daughters, Dalia and Hadar, the lights of his life, busily preparing the evening meal.

They didn't know what he did with the days and nights he was away from them—he took care they didn't, always giving them a plausible reason. He told them he was traveling to another town to barter for the leather needed to make the belts that provided them a living, or was staying with a sick friend—anything but what he was really doing. His gentle wife would be horrified that he'd become an assassin, even though she agreed with the patriots in theory. And his daughters were only ten and three years old, much too young to know the sordid details of how to bring a corrupt government to its knees.

He sighed as he came within sight of their home on the outskirts of the Lower City. It looked like many other homes nearby—stone walls surrounding an inner open courtyard. He knew Adina was probably cooking their supper on the open fire in the center of that courtyard. He heard the bleat of the goats corralled inside in a small stall where they would spend the night. Their home wasn't large, but it was filled with joy and love for each other—no price was too much to pay for that. But Barabbas's mind was conflicted.

So many secrets—it wasn't what he wanted for them. But it was necessary, he'd come to believe, to provide for their future. Rome was a vicious, unconscionable taskmaster, and Rome's tool, the Jewish priest-rulers, were no better. *The sooner the Jews could rule themselves the better. It's too bad we must do it this way, but there is no other way.*

As he approached their home, the sound of giggling reached his ears. He stopped, playing their game as he always did. He looked this way and that, pushed aside a rock, lifted the branch of a bush. He crept over to the stone wall of the house and peered around the corner. The giggling intensified. Then without warning a small tornado took him, almost toppling him, resolving itself into his two small girls.

Shrieking with laughter, they ran around him in circles as he pretended to try to catch them. Finally reaching out with lightning speed, he caught them up in his strong arms and swung them around and around until they begged him to stop. It was the same every time he came home, and he lived for it. These two, and Adina, now standing framed in the doorway, were infinitely worth the separation, the danger, the secret life he lived.

"Oh, Barabbas! You're home!" Adina said, her beautiful eyes shining. "Come in. Come in. I have supper almost prepared."

"I'll be there soon, my dear. Please wait until I go have a wash. I'm not fit for civilized company just yet," Barabbas replied. He turned to go around to the back of their home, where a small creek meandered its way toward the outer wall of the city. Dalia and Hadar still clung to him and made as if to follow him, but he waved them toward their mother.

"No, girls, go inside with your mother. I'll be along in a moment," he commanded, not wanting them to watch him "have a wash." They obediently let go of him and ran inside the house.

Barabbas went to the creek, washed his hands and face, and then carefully removed the sica from under his cloak. Plunging it under the flowing water, he watched the man's blood drift away from him. For a moment he felt sadness—at what, he didn't know. Eldad had deserved his fate, but a part of Barabbas regretted what had to be done. Barabbas thought to pray for the man and his family, but he had no one to pray to.

***

Later that evening Barabbas and Adina sat on their small porch watching Dalia and Hadar play in the waning light.

They giggled and chased each other around in circles, each trying to drop a bug on the other's head. Finally, Hadar shrieked as Dalia ran up behind her and dropped a bright yellow beetle into her hair. The insect quickly became entangled, buzzing and squirming as it tried to spread its wings and fly away. Its efforts were hampered as Hadar leaned over and frantically shook her head, using both hands to try to brush it out. Dalia collapsed on the hard-packed dirt and laughed at her younger sister until the tears were flowing.

Hadar ran to the porch for rescue. Barabbas grasped her long locks and pulled the bug out of her hair. Hadar shrank back as he held it out to her, then leaped off the porch as the game began all over again. Barabbas and Adina laughed together at their antics. Barabbas reveled in the sweetness of the evening and the closeness of his family.

Yes, this is what I live for. This moment, right here, makes it all worth it.

Barabbas leaned closer to Adina, taking her delicate hand in his large one.

"Husband, did you hear what happened today?" she asked him quietly. Barabbas was immediately on the alert. He instinctively knew what her news was. It had been several months since there'd been any killings in the city—most happened out in the countryside—and news traveled fast.

"No," he said as nonchalantly as he could muster, "what happened?"

" A man was murdered right in the middle of the marketplace at midday," she whispered.

"Oh?" He tried to look concerned to allay her suspicion. Adina searched his face.

"They say he carried gold paid to him by Rome for giving up the names of those two patriots who were burned and crucified."

Barabbas watched his daughters intently as Adina watched

him.

"They?"

"The neighbors who carried this gossip to me—you know who I mean. I went to the market today with the girls. Everyone was talking about it."

"Adina, when were you there? Did it happen while you were there?"

"Oh, no. I was there at about the ninth hour. We'd grown tired of waiting for you to come home. We didn't need anything; I just wanted to distract the girls—they were growing impatient to see you."

Barabbas relaxed. Dalia and Hadar were now sitting in the dirt, chasing their beetles with sticks, making them run. His eyes misted over at their innocent play.

"Barabbas, you don't look surprised," Adina said, dragging him out of his reverie.

"Surprised?"

"Yes, surprised. Did you hear about it also?"

"No, I didn't." *At least it's the truth,* he thought.

"And you're not surprised?" she persisted.

"No, I'm not, Adina," he said, turning to look at her. "Rome is always paying traitorous collaborators, and then the traitors get themselves killed. This is the way it is and will continue to be until we finally rid ourselves of the lot of them—Rome and their conspirators who serve in our temple."

Adina slowly slipped her hand out of his and turned her attention to their children. She was silent, worry lines deepening on her face. Barabbas reached out and smoothed a stray hair from her face, and then placing his rough hand gently under her chin, he turned her face to his. Her frightened gaze met his.

"My dear, don't take it to heart so. You know…you agree, don't you, that this war must continue until we are victorious? Or have you forgotten our history? The Maccabees—Mattathias and his sons—sacrificed themselves to throw off the Seleucid armies and the degradation of the Greeks, refusing to obey the decree of Antiochus. We must honor their sacrifice by continuing their fight for the freedom of our people. You do agree, don't you? You're with me in this—please tell me you agree."

"I used to, husband. I still do."

She turned from him again, watching the sun sink below the horizon. "But what of our family? I honor the sacrifice of those brave men, but it's a small thing when I look at our precious girls. They, and you, Barabbas, are my life!"

She suddenly turned to him, a look of fierce determination glowing out of her eyes. "Barabbas, you had nothing to do with it! Tell me now you had nothing to do with it," she demanded.

Barabbas sighed. Another lie must be told to this woman who had already been told so many. He put his arm around her and drew her close to him. Her sweet smell always intoxicated him, and now was no different, despite their argument.

"No, sweetheart, I had nothing to do with it. I promise," he said into her hair. He felt her sag against him in relief. In his mind's eye, he saw the blood drifting from his blade, following the swift-flowing water of the creek, and he knew he would feel the guilt of this false promise for the rest of his life.

The apostle Paul, in Romans 7:24–25, laments the human condition—the continual juxtaposition of the law and God's mercy, the struggle of the new nature against the old.

> Oh, what a miserable person I am! Who will free me
> from this life that is dominated by sin and death?
> Thank God! The answer is in Jesus Christ our Lord. So you
> see how it is: In my mind I really want to obey God's law,
> but because of my sinful nature I am a slave to sin.

Barabbas faces the same struggle. He fights for the freedom

of his people, a noble cause, but by means that God despises—murder, which sends His beloved creatures into eternity with no chance to know Him.

On some level, Barabbas knows his life has gone astray, but we must remember he hasn't met Jesus yet. God is working in the background to arrange that divine appointment, to bring Barabbas to the point of the precipice where he must choose heaven or hell as his eternal dwelling place—the same precipice to which He draws you inexorably, where you must choose life with God or life without God.

They came for him in the night.

Barabbas awoke to the screams of Adina and the sound of shuffling feet on their sleeping room floor. He'd been slumbering so soundly after his four-day ordeal that he'd heard nothing amiss. He rolled quickly off the mat he and Adina slept on, slipping his hand under it in a smooth motion to grip his blade. Only then did he focus on the scene before him.

The sight that met his eyes caused the bile to rise in his throat, and he almost vomited.

One soldier had Adina by the hair and groped her as she sobbed and frantically cried out Barabbas's name. Another held Dalia and Hadar in his massive grip, leering crudely at the two frightened little girls.

He stood up quickly, blade at the ready. It flashed in the moonlight streaming through the small window as he took a menacing step toward the armed men crowding into the small room. Barabbas was a big man and could easily subdue two, even three Roman soldiers single handedly, but not when they held his family in their grips.

"I wouldn't if I were you," warned the soldier who held his girls.

Barabbas tightened his grip on his blade as the soldier

wrapped his huge hand around Dalia's neck. He knew the soldier could snap it with very little effort. His blade clattered to the floor as Barabbas slid to his knees.

"Barabbas!" Adina sobbed. "What's happening?"

Receiving a vicious slap from her captor, she quieted to a whimper, her eyes twin pools of fright, cheeks wet with tears. Barabbas didn't answer her, just looked at her sorrowfully as two men rushed him, one grasping his shoulder and the other jerking his head back by the hair.

The brute holding Adina grabbed her chin and tilted her face up to his.

"Now, where was I?" he growled, face inches from hers. She struggled against him, causing him to break into peals of laughter, joined by the other soldiers.

Agonized and out of his mind with fear for her, Barabbas used all his strength in a sudden move, breaking the grip of the two who held him. Stiff-arming one, he sent the soldier flying backward; the other received a massive blow to his forehead by Barabbas's huge fist. That one dropped, rolled, and crashed into the other.

Barabbas took a step toward Adina, then another, but was viciously clubbed on the back of his neck from behind. He dropped like a stone, moaning in pain. Rolling over, he was met with the point of a sword barely an inch from his right eye. He froze.

"Look well, my friend. This is the last vision you will have of her," sneered the soldier who held Adina, now sobbing uncontrollably. Dalia and Hadar stood silent, statue-like, frozen in fear. Barabbas closed his eyes against the horrific sight of his wife and daughters being treated like animals. Hatred crashed through his chest, threatening to suffocate him. He lay there, seemingly docile, planning his next move.

I will kill them – I will not let even one of them live, he vowed to himself.

Suddenly the confrontation was over as the Roman commander stepped heavily into the room, followed by his officers.

"Enough!" he shouted at his men. "Let the women go—it's him we want."

"But, sir, they could be used as leverage, to make him talk," said the soldier holding Adina, ogling her. "And for other uses," he added with a nasty sneer.

His commander brandished his sword at him.

"I said, enough! Let her go, or I'll run you through here and now!"

The soldier obeyed immediately, throwing her to the floor, where she scrabbled frantically to Barabbas. The commander stepped over to Barabbas and hauled him to his feet, hindered by Adina as she tightly grasped her husband's legs.

Barabbas bent over and unwound her arms, whispering in her ear.

"I'm so sorry, my dear one. I'm so sorry."

His daughters had been released, and now they wrapped their arms around their parents with heartbreaking sobs. Barabbas pried their hands from him and pushed them into Adina's trembling arms as she still knelt at his feet.

"Take care of my girls, dearest one," Barabbas whispered as the soldiers secured his hands behind his back and shackled his ankles.

The last sight of his family, as he was driven out of his home into that blackest of nights, was Adina kneeling on the bedroom floor with his precious girls clinging to her. He knew he would never forget the sound of their weeping.

***

Barabbas was taken to a small Jerusalem jail nearby. After walking, surrounded by sixteen Roman soldiers, through the tunnels under the jailer's house, he was unshackled and shoved into a hole in the floor, dropping a good twelve feet to land in a pile of human excrement. He cleaned himself up as best he could, stoically holding off the tears, and then crept to a corner that was relatively dry. He heard the tramp of feet as the squad of soldiers left him, their laughter drifting to his ears.

Darkness blanketed Barabbas, blinding him so he couldn't see his hand in front of his face. In the heavy silence, he could hear the shuffling of tiny feet. *Rats will be my new companions*, he thought with a shudder. He could never abide rats. He looked up to the hole in the ceiling through which he'd been dropped—not even a glimmer of light up there either.

Barabbas had been told he would see the magistrate in the morning. He knew what that meant. He would be convicted—without a trial—of insurrection and murder, and then hanged, or worse. Traitors to the Roman Empire suffered the most barbarous of executions. His eyes filled with those held-off tears as he contemplated his end. He wasn't so concerned about himself. He couldn't bear to think how Adina and his daughters would suffer.

What have I done? Adina will never forgive me for abandoning her in my selfish, patriotic pride. What will happen to them? How will they eat?

He knew what kind of life a single mother must lead. She would likely become the slave of some wealthy Roman brute, along with the girls...*oh, I can't bear it. I can't bear it!* His mind screamed at him, remembering the sobs of his family as he was driven from their home.

He now knew Adina was right and he'd been wrong. He should have left off his zealot activities and concentrated on being a good husband and father. Instead, he was now stuck with his choices and the brutal consequences. He would pay the ultimate price, and there would be no help for him—or for his beloved girls.

He desperately needed sleep, but none would come. He tried to adjust himself into a more comfortable position, pillowing his head on his hands, but the foul odor of the floor coupled with the sounds and shadowy movement of the rodents across the room would not allow him to relax.

He sat up again, leaning against the damp stone wall, and bowed his head. He prayed, but he realized he was the only audience to his prayers—himself and the rats. His tears fell afresh as he knew, once again, he had no one to pray to, no one who would listen to him, no one who could help him. Desperation and despair crashed through his chest, causing physical pain. The strong Jewish patriot who'd schemed with others to bring about the downfall of Rome and hypocritical priestly rule, who had once single handedly fought off four tough Roman soldiers who were abusing a compatriot, was now reduced to an insignificant cog in the wheel of the Roman machine, headed for a traitor's death.

There is no god. If there was, he would help me. But why would he? I'm a murderer, a traitor, and an unfit father and husband. Why would he?

With those thoughts swirling through his head, Barabbas finally fell into a fitful doze, his head tilted back against the stone wall, arms wrapped tightly around himself.

The expression "my prayers don't go past the ceiling" is a common one. In the depths of despair, we'd like to feel that our anguished cries for help are listened to by someone who can bring relief. I've been there, and I bet you have too.

Barabbas sits in a dark prison of his own making. He realizes he can't blame anyone but himself. His life is littered with dead bodies, stolen money, neglected family, and lies. What god would possibly accept him, let alone help him. Far worse than the pile of excrement into which he was thrown are the miserable doubts that assail him.

Barabbas knows his end, as we all instinctively do when faced with our own rebellion and unbelief. Barabbas has, as we have, a God-shaped hole in his heart that remains unfilled.

God longs to fill the hole in Barabbas's heart with Himself, completely and fully—as He longs to fill the hole in your heart. God will shift the heavens to make that happen, for Barabbas and for you.

As Barabbas miserably contemplates paying the ultimate price for his sins, God watches—and contemplates the plan already in play that will certainly turn the world upside down. And unknowingly, Barabbas has a box seat.

The next day, Barabbas was hauled out of his hole by a rope and taken to the magistrate. It went as expected—he was identified by an eyewitness as the murderer of Eldad. More witnesses were called who told of his subversive activities—some true, some false, all damning. He was sentenced to the traitor's death—thirty-nine lashes with the cat-o'-nine-tails and crucifixion—to be carried out on the morrow. He doubted he'd live through the flogging.

The magistrate asked Barabbas if he wanted to see his family.

"No," he replied. He would not put Adina and his little girls through that.

He was then taken, mercifully, to a cell near the Antonian fortress in the northwest corner of the Temple Mount. It was cleaner there, much warmer, and he could at least have light and hear people talking and laughing, albeit Roman voices. He was quite alone—there was an unoccupied cell next to him.

Barabbas dozed a little throughout that day, still racked with grief whenever his thoughts drifted homeward.

At midday, they brought food to him—passable, but unidentifiable food—throwing it through the bars onto the floor. He'd had nothing to eat since dinner at home almost two days ago, so he didn't much care what it was or how it was served. He ate every scrap.

The hours wore on. The forced idleness, filled only with thoughts of home, almost drove him over the edge of madness. No supper was served. He wished he'd saved a bit of the midday meal. No matter—nothing mattered to him anymore but getting this wretched business over with. He fell into a fitful sleep around midnight, with visions of the flogging to come in the morning and of hanging on a tree in the dung heap just outside the city. He fervently hoped Adina would stay away.

***

Barabbas awoke to the sound of marching. *Already?* But they were not coming for him. They surrounded a badly beaten man, shoving him along in front of them and throwing him into the adjoining cell. The man looked barely alive, blood flowing from several wounds, robe torn and hanging in shreds from his back. He groaned as he was roughly pushed into the cell, landing on his side, his face away from Barabbas.

Barabbas didn't recognize the man—he clearly wasn't part of Barabbas's small band of subversives.

Poor slob, he thought. *Probably a peasant in the wrong place at the wrong time.*

One of the soldiers glanced over at Barabbas and whispered, "Reprieve, my friend, reprieve. Your execution, although richly deserved, will be delayed until we deal with this scum. But don't get too comfortable—you will surely hang, and soon."

The troop of soldiers marched out, leaving Barabbas alone with the prisoner next to him.

The man lay there, breathing heavily, groaning from time to time. Barabbas watched him as he rolled over on the hard-packed dirt. As he turned over, his face came into view, and Barabbas blanched. It hardly looked human. Swollen jaw, eyes bloody, smashed cheekbone, and the punctures on his forehead looked curiously like small snakebites. Barabbas wondered what the man had done to warrant such abuse.

"Sir," Barabbas whispered. "What is your name? Sir?"

The man did not stir, so Barabbas gave up the attempt. *Maybe the man would die here, next to him, before the soldiers could continue their beatings and abuse. That would be a mercy.*

Barabbas, with nothing else to do, was soon lulled into sleep, listening to the soft, rattled breathing of his companion. He dreamed again of Adina, of the nights of loving her, of the days of deceiving her, of her heart breaking because of him. In his dream he once again played hide and seek with his girls; he heard them giggle and reached for them. They escaped just out of his grasp and ran away. He followed, looking under furniture, on the back porch of their home, out at the empty landscape. He saw them in the distance, running away from him. He called to them. They turned toward him, stretching out their arms, but then they melted away as if they'd never been. He turned frantically back toward the house and sobbed as he saw Adina reaching for him, racked with grief, accusation in her eyes, and then she too faded away from his sight as if she'd never existed, her shimmering form growing dimmer, dimmer, and then disappearing altogether. He dropped to his knees in shame, collapsing to his back in the dirt, sobbing his grief to an empty sky.

***

Barabbas awoke, stiff from lying on his back all night, still a prisoner of Rome and the Jewish authorities, still in his jail cell—but now something was different. He judged it to be about three hours before dawn. He could hear the whispering of men somewhere in the dark and then loud laughter.

"Well, which one do you think it will be, friend? The murderer or the so-called blasphemer?" queried a rough voice.

"I don't know! How should I know? Who do you think it will be?"

Silence followed the question.

Barabbas strained to hear the answer.

"I don't much care, do you? Does it really matter which Barabbas we hang?"

What a curious thing to say! This man's name is Barabbas, like me? Barabbas looked over at the man in the next cell and was surprised to see him sitting up and staring at him. Barabbas drug himself closer to the bars separating them. He stared into the man's face, noting much of the swelling had gone down and the rivers of blood had dried on the man's cheeks. The silence stretched as they took each other's measure. Finally, Barabbas spoke first.

"Is your name Barabbas?" he asked, hands clinging to the bars.

"No, my friend," the voice rasped out between broken teeth. "It's Jesus."

"Jesus? But they just said..." Barabbas began.

Jesus interrupted him. "I'm a woodworker from Nazareth." He moved closer to the bars. Scarcely a foot separated them.

"Nazareth?" Barabbas asked.

Jesus nodded, his eyes boring into Barabbas's.

"You're not...you're not that man who's been going around preaching and healing, are you?" Barabbas asked, astonished.

Jesus smiled at him. "Yes, my friend, I am he. Are you surprised?"

"Well...yes, yes, I am," Barabbas sputtered. "I've heard you claim to be a god or something. If you are, how can you be here, a prisoner like me, condemned to die?"

Jesus, unhurried, allowed silence to permeate the cell for several moments before answering.

"Your name is Barabbas. *Son of a father*. You have a good wife, Adina, and two of the most delightful little girls ever made by God—Dalia and Hadar. You're a leatherworker with great talent. You suffer because you have no one to pray to," Jesus said.

Barabbas gasped. "But—"

"You are also the murderer of Eldad," Jesus finished.

At that Barabbas clutched at the bars between them, white knuckled.

"Who are you?" Barabbas demanded. "A spy? Why are you here? Have you been paid by Rome to make me confess to something?" Barabbas's anger and confusion mounted—he wanted to reach through the bars and strangle the man where he sat.

"Who am I?" Jesus asked softly. "Who am I? I am son of the

Father—*the* Father. That's why the soldiers called us both Barabbas."

Barabbas sagged against the moist wall at his back.

"You're crazy," he mumbled. "I've heard you claim to be able to raise the dead, tear down our temple and build it again in three days. You consort with the most unsavory of characters—people your supposed god wouldn't have anything to do with. I've heard your followers are illiterate fishermen, just as crazy and marked for death as you are. And you call yourself the son of a god! If you were, you wouldn't be here…do you hear me? You wouldn't be here!" Barabbas, spent with the effort of his anger, fell into silence.

The soft answer came out of the lightening darkness.

"I'm here for you, Barabbas."

Barabbas laughed shrilly.

"For me? No one's for me. I've done my bit for my people, and look where it got me! I'll never…I'll never…" Barabbas choked, unable to continue.

"See Adina again? Hold her close? Protect her and your little ones? Watch them grow up? Make a son with Adina?" Jesus finished his sentence.

Barabbas stared at Jesus. Then the words came rushing out. He was as unable to stop them as he was unable to stop what was happening to him. "See? You're crazy! Gods don't talk like that!" Barabbas wagged his head back and forth in frustration. "Why do you talk to me like this? If you're a god, and you know my heart, why don't you get us both out of here? Why don't you help me?" Barabbas turned his back, hunching down in grief.

"I do know your heart, Barabbas. And I'm here because my Father put me here."

Barabbas turned at that. "Humph! Some father you have then—why would he do that?"

"Oh, Barabbas, there's so much you don't understand now. But you will, my friend. You will," Jesus said in a whisper. And then silence fell again. Jesus relaxed back against the wall, lips moving, a faraway look in his eyes. Barabbas finally turned from him, weakly allowing his body to slump sideways, his grief torturing him again.

"I do know your heart, Barabbas."

God's knowledge of His creatures is complete. He knows me, and He knows you. He thought tenderly and passionately of us before the foundations of the earth were set, planning even then for our redemption in Christ Jesus:

> He [Christ] will strike your [Satan's] head,
> And you [Satan] will strike his [Christ's] heel.
> (Genesis 3:15)

> O Lord, you have examined my heart and know everything about me. You made all the delicate, inner parts of my body and knit me together in my mother's womb.
> You watched me as I was being formed in utter seclusion, as I was woven together in the dark of the womb. You saw me before I was born. Every day of my life was recorded in your book. Every moment was laid out before a single day had passed.
> How precious are your thoughts about me, O God. They cannot be numbered!
> (Psalm 139:1, 13, 15–17)

God created us with a longing to be fully known. That's why friendships and fellowship are so central to the human experience. That's why betrayal is so excruciating. It's interesting to note that the root word of excruciating is *crux*, or cross, and means to torture or to torment.

No one can fully know us but God. When I bare my soul to Him Who tenderly watches me, zealously protects me, and faithfully guides me through this life and into the next, I am fully satisfied as I can be with no other.

He's as close as my next heartbeat, my next breath—He lives just under my skin. His shoulders are so massive that they carried the weight of the entire world's sins all the way to the cross—I know they can bear the weight of my sorrows. I know He hears every whisper in the dark, sees every teardrop fall, knows every anxious, unspoken thought.

Will my children follow Jesus after I'm gone?

What will dying be like?

Why must children suffer?

Are my sister and brother with You? Will I see them again?

Is that grievous sin I committed so long ago *really* forgiven? Or the sin to which I surrender even now, over and over again?

Will the world survive our petty differences, our wars, the rampant evil permeating every corner of the planet?

Will I have enough money to live on if he dies?

These are but a few of my anxious thoughts. God is the only One of whom I can say, "He knows me." Can you say the same? Dear reader, are you sitting today in a prison, unable to perceive your prayers making it past the ceiling, tormented by the thought that no one is there to hear?

Jesus *is* there—pleading with the Father for you, claiming you as His own, longing for you to know and trust Him with your anxious thoughts. Have you lifted your soul to His throne, laid your heartaches, fears, and failures in His lap?

He waits for you now.

"Husband, I beg of you—have nothing to do with him. He has spoken to me," Claudia whispered. Dawn was just peeping over the horizon. Pilate was surprised his wife was up so early—she never made her picture-perfect appearance until midmorning. But now she paced their sitting room, disheveled as a street woman, dark circles under her eyes, hands trembling at her sides.

Pontius Pilate—fifth prefect of the Roman province of Judea, serving under Emperor Tiberius—was astonished at his wife's words.

"What are you talking about? And speak up, wife. I can't hear you when you buzz in my ear like that!" Pilate grumbled disagreeably.

He was in a foul mood. He deeply resented being away from his home in Caesarea, having come to Jerusalem during the Jews' Passover celebration in order to keep the peace. *And, it seemed, there would be no peace* this *year, thanks to this rabble-rouser, Jesus of Nazareth.*

And now even his wife was disturbed about this Jewish peasant he'd had arrested and thrown into jail. He'd never understand these Jews. Their religious hierarchy alone was enough to boggle the mind—and so many rules. No wonder the people were always in revolt and in need of peacekeeping.

He turned to his wife again.

"Now, my dear," he began again, trying to be kind, "what was it you were saying?" He lifted his large hand and swatted a fly. *Infernal insects! At least in Caesarea I have servants around me who keep the rooms free of them—here, my household is reduced by half.*

"That man who calls himself the king of the Jews. I've had a nightmare about him. He spoke to me, husband. I tell you—he spoke to me!"

Pilate considered Claudia's words, disliking them heartily. He couldn't abide her histrionics, and he'd already come to the conclusion that this so-called king of the Jews was innocent of plotting against Rome, but he didn't like to be told by his wife what to do.

"Spoke to you? What did he say?"

Claudia turned away for a moment, clearly trying to control her emotion.

"Come, wife...what did he say? He's a peasant, one of these

'messiahs' running around confusing the commoners. What could he possibly have said to you—in a dream, no less—that would frighten you so?"

Claudia had been pacing while Pilate spoke. Now she stopped directly in front of him, and with eyes glittering she said shakily, "This is what he said to me: 'I know you, Claudia. I was there when your parents conceived you. I was there when you were born, when you suffered under your uncle's hand, when your dear mother was killed. I was there that night you cried into your pillow after being given away to be married when you were thirteen. Claudia, I know you, and you are loved with an everlasting love.'"

She stopped abruptly, hands shaking, hair falling into her face. She nervously picked at the sleeve of her gown as she awaited his answer. Pilate had never seen her like this—her self-control was legendary. This unrestrained agitation unnerved him, rendering him speechless.

"Husband! What have you to say?" Claudia demanded.

"What do you want me to say? I must do my duty, wife!" Pilate arose and walked to the open doorway across the large room. He peered out, and, seeing no one lurking in the passageway, closed the door and turned around. He scowled at his wife.

"I don't understand, Claudia. Are you sure that's what he said? How could he possibly know you? And how could he have spoken these words in a dream? It's nonsense!" Pilate was a practical man—dreams did not impress him.

"That's what he said," she insisted. "Have nothing to do with this innocent man…I plead with you! He's more than just a man, more than just another false messiah. I believe he is who he says he is, and if you don't let him go, his death will be on your head."

Pilate didn't answer her, just stared. Finally, without another word, Claudia turned and walked quickly away. Pilate watched her reach the door, open it, and go out without so much as a backward glance. Shaking his head, he stepped to the balcony just off their sitting room, where his seat of judgment overlooked the public square.

Eyes narrowed against the brightness of the morning sun, he scrutinized the gathering crowd, noting Jewish council members scattered among the throng of peasants. He'd have to make a decision soon if he was to circumvent an uprising, something to be avoided at all costs. The emperor didn't like riots in these outlying provinces, and he'd be shuttled off to some dusty little town in a heartbeat if he couldn't keep order here in Jerusalem. Pilate felt a throbbing pain in his head at the thought.

"You!" he hissed angrily at the servant standing in the shadows.

The man scurried forward and bowed.

"Get me some water," Pilate ordered. "And bring my physician. Tell him I have a pain in my head and I'm in need of a potion." The servant hurried away.

Pilate sat heavily on the wide stone seat, gazing with unseeing eyes over the heads of the busy street. *This will end badly if I'm not careful.*

***

The midday meal was served in the same fashion as the day before—thrown through the bars and landing on the floor. Both Barabbas and Jesus grabbed and ate. Barabbas noticed Jesus had some trouble getting the food down past his broken teeth and cheek bones, but he managed to swallow most of it. Then with nothing else to do, they both crawled over to sit, supported by the wall at their backs, bars separating them. Silence descended, broken only by an occasional laugh in the distance.

Finally, Barabbas couldn't tolerate the silence anymore. He remembered the last words Jesus spoke to him—*there's so much you don't understand now. But you will, my friend. You will*—and he wanted to know his meaning.

Not that it will make any difference, but at least talking will pass the time, even if I'm talking to a crazy man.

"Sir, what did you mean before, that 'there's so much I don't understand, but I will'? What don't I understand?"

Jesus looked away from Barabbas for a moment. He cocked his head, as if listening to the distant sound of their jailers talking and laughing. Then as he turned his head to look at Barabbas, his movement was arrested, eyes focused across his cell. Barabbas followed his gaze. A rat, the biggest Barabbas had ever seen, thick-tailed, eyed Jesus. Jesus stared at the rat, and the rat stared back. Jesus held out his hand. The rat shuffled leisurely to Jesus, who held his hand palm up near the dusty floor.

Fascinated, Barabbas watched the drama, his question forgotten for the moment.

The rat reached the hand of Jesus, hesitated, smelled his fingertips, then jumped into his palm. Jesus brought his hand to his lap, watching as the large rodent scrutinized him. Then the rat flopped over on its side, curled itself into a tight ball, and closed its eyes. Jesus petted it for a moment, then gently lowered his hand—the rat sleeping peacefully in his palm—to his lap. He turned his attention back to Barabbas.

Barabbas swallowed hard, eyes glued to Jesus's hand.

"Yes, Barabbas, there is much you do not understand. May I ask you a question?" Jesus said, now covering the rat with his other hand as it slept.

For a moment Barabbas was speechless. The rats Barabbas had known were more apt to chew on a person, not obediently lay in the hand and sleep.

"Barabbas? May I ask you a question?" Jesus repeated. "We'll talk about my friend here in just a moment if you want," he said with a grin, then grimacing, his facial injuries clearly painful.

Barabbas nodded, unable to pry his eyes away from Jesus's hands. *Who was he?* For a moment, Barabbas had to fight off the longing to change places with the rat.

"Barabbas, for what do you fight?" Jesus asked.

Barabbas shifted his focus. "I fight for the freedom of my people," Barabbas declared with passion.

"Excellent!" Jesus exclaimed. "So do I!"

"You?" Barabbas questioned, stumbling over his words. "I haven't seen you among the patriots. Do you have your own group, a secret one? Have you had any success getting rid of our enemies? Tell me about the group you fight with."

Jesus smiled at him indulgently. "Barabbas, the freedom I fight for is not the freedom you fight for. I like your fire and passion though." Jesus paused, then said, "And here's another question. Which is better—to kill your enemy or to turn your enemy into a friend?"

"I'd rather get rid of my enemies than try to convert them. They don't convert easily, in my experience."

"Yes, I know what you mean. Some enemies are very stubborn," Jesus said enigmatically, his gaze piercing. Barabbas felt uncomfortable under that gaze, averting his eyes once again to the rat's cradle.

"But, Jesus, what kind of freedom are you fighting for? Do you not hate the rule of the Romans and the priests?"

"Oh yes, I agree with you, Barabbas—the Romans do not rule with true justice, and the priests have so perverted the Law of Moses that it turns the stomach."

"But...I don't understand, Jesus. What freedom are you talking about then?"

"The only true freedom there is, my friend. Freedom from the tyranny of the only real enemy in this world—that old devil, the serpent, the adversary of my Father in heaven."

Barabbas wasn't impressed with this statement. "Well, you can fight all you want against 'the devil.' I'd rather bloody the enemy I can see," he said emphatically.

"Then, my friend, you will lose your soul. What do you benefit if you gain the whole world but lose your own soul? Is anything worth more than your soul?"

Those words calmly spoken by Jesus flowed over his mind, destroyed his arguments, rebuilt his thoughts, shifted his perspective. It was as if he walked out of his prison cell, heavy with darkness, into a wide vista of light, blazing and warm.

"Yes, my friend, that's it. You're there, aren't you? That is the freedom for which I fight. Now you must choose to stay," Jesus said softly.

His face was a puzzle—Barabbas couldn't read it. As he considered Jesus's words, Jesus uncovered the rat in his palm. It rolled over, sat up, and opened its eyes. The creature stood on its hind legs, motionless in Jesus's palm except for its twitching nose. Jesus and the rat eyed each other. A smile played around Jesus's mouth. The rat then turned its head and looked at Barabbas with his beady eyes, holding his gaze for an astonishing moment. Barabbas thought he saw the rat's eyes twinkle. Then the rat turned his gaze back to Jesus.

I would swear they're communicating in some way. Impossible! And yet…

Then Jesus lowered his hand to the floor, and the rat climbed down and trekked slowly to the other side of the cell, its rump and tail swaying from side to side.

Barabbas and Jesus watched it slowly arrive at a small hole in the wall and then turn and look back at Jesus. It stood on its hind feet again for a moment, head raised in their direction. Barabbas now watched Jesus's face. He was dumbfounded to see the same knowing in his face as when Jesus looked at *him*, Barabbas. A moment passed, and then the rat fell to all fours and disappeared into the hole. Barabbas shook his head in disbelief.

"Another enemy converted, my friend," Jesus said.

Barabbas had no words. *What just happened?*

"Barabbas," he said matter of factly, "I've known that rat for a long time—just as I've known you for a long time. Here's the truth: My Father in heaven has sent me from his side to secure freedom for all people. And he placed me here with you, in this jail, for one reason. To make a friend of an enemy."

Barabbas was silent, confused. There was no escape from Jesus's burning gaze or his words. Barabbas pressed his face into the bars, gripping them again.

"I'm not your enemy," he said gruffly. "Why do you call me that?"

"Because you're not my friend. With me, there is no in-between. Barabbas, do you believe in God?"

"Well…of course…I…well, doesn't everybody? What kind of question is that? Of course I believe in God!" Barabbas exclaimed.

A huge smile split Jesus's face. "Excellent!" he said for the second time.

"Barabbas, do you believe God?" Jesus asked quietly.

"But, Jesus, I just told you…" Barabbas began.

"No, Barabbas. I ask now if you *believe God*—believe who he is, what he says. Do you? That's a much different question than the first one. Saying you believe *in* God demands no obedience, no commitment from you."

"I…I don't know," Barabbas said, quite miserable to admit that. "You speak as if God is a person, someone who's watching, listening, right *here*. I guess I don't know who he is or what he's said."

"He is a real person, and he is right here. And he has said this, Barabbas: you are loved, completely, fully. You're drenched in His love, Barabbas. You are speaking now to his love. God's love sits with you in this jail, awaiting judgment, just like you," Jesus said, now with *his* face pressed against the bars in his passion. "Barabbas, do you understand what I'm saying?"

Wide-eyed, Barabbas stammered, "Are you…are you saying you are…God?"

"Yes, Barabbas. And what's more, you will see the judge of the earth step down from his seat of judgment and become the judged. For you, Barabbas. The innocent will be condemned, and you, the guilty, will go free," Jesus whispered.

Barabbas couldn't move, couldn't speak.

"Barabbas, do you believe?" Jesus asked him again, urgently now.

Barabbas, his whole body and mind trembling now, could not answer. He wanted to, oh, how he wanted to! But his mind could not grasp the enormity of what Jesus said. *God judged by this corrupt world? God condemned by his own guilt-ridden creatures? It makes no sense!*

"It makes no sense from your point of view, but it makes perfect sense from mine. Let me ask a question. Would you gladly exchange places with your sweet little daughter, Hadar, if she was accused and sentenced to death?"

Barabbas, white faced, spluttered, "Of course I would! I don't even have to think about it!"

Jesus nodded his head. "I knew you would say that. But, Barabbas, here's the thing. I am doing the same for you, right now. You're powerless against the adversary—I am not. He will bruise my heel this day, but I will crush his head, and in so doing, I will kill death forever," Jesus whispered passionately.

Barabbas sagged against the cell wall, undone by this strange conversation. His mind was in turmoil. He wanted—he needed—to think. To make sense of it. He who had spent his life working and fighting for freedom was now a prisoner condemned to die. But in the next cell was one who promised him freedom—himself a prisoner!

What can Jesus do to get me out?

Head pounding, he leaned sideways against the bars and closed his eyes, shutting out the sight of the beaten man who promised freedom. Soon he was asleep, his questions swirling like buzzards in his thoughts even as he slept.

***

They came for him in the hour before the dawn. Rough hands dragged him from his sleep. They spit on him, hit him across the back with the flat of a sword, kicked him when he stumbled, cursed him when he groaned in pain.

Barabbas awoke with a jolt, watching the soldiers abuse Jesus. He couldn't speak. He sat frozen in fear.

Jesus lay close to the bars, moaning in pain as they kicked

him again and again. One brute brought his sword point to Jesus's neck and pressed, drawing blood. Then he reached down and smeared the trickle of blood across Jesus's face, chortling as he painted a picture of a rough cross on his cheek.

Barabbas, unable to stop himself, screamed at the soldier in fury.

"Stop! Stop. I beg of you! He's down, you idiot. He's down! What more can you do to him?" Barabbas gripped the bar with one hand, reaching through with the other to grasp the shoulder of Jesus.

Jesus opened one eye and gazed at Barabbas, saying something. Barabbas, hand still on Jesus's shoulder, leaned down to hear what he said.

"My friend, let me be. It must be so," Jesus whispered. "My Father in heaven has ordained your rescue and that of the whole world."

"This can't be the way, Jesus. Why does it have to be like this? You're innocent!"

Jesus shook his head, groaning. "But you're *not* innocent, Barabbas," he rasped. "It must be this way for your rescue. You can't rescue yourself. I must do it for you."

Barabbas shook his head, agonized over Jesus's suffering. He tightened his grip on Jesus, squeezing his eyes shut against the pain in Jesus's eyes.

This can't be the way. What kind of father are you?

The soldier brought the flat of his sword down on Barabbas's wrist, breaking it with an audible crack. Grinning as Barabbas cried out in agony and tucked his injured arm to himself, the soldier said, face inches from Barabbas's, "What more can we do to him? You will see, scum, and then you will see what more we can do to you."

They dragged Jesus by the hair out of Barabbas's reach, then jerked him to his feet. As they reached the cell door, Jesus turned shakily and looked at Barabbas. A look of sorrow, of grief, of question spread across Jesus's face.

"For you, Barabbas, for you," Jesus whispered.

Barabbas leaned his forehead against the bars and broke into loud sobs.

The soldier nearest Barabbas reached through the bars and grabbed his hair, first jerking his head back and then viciously slamming his head against the bars. "Shut up, scum! Unless you want me to gut you here and now!"

Barabbas swallowed his sobs.

"Barabbas, will you believe?" Jesus asked.

Barabbas stared in anguish, unable to speak. And with a final brutal shove, Jesus disappeared into the outer corridor with the soldiers.

Several moments passed. Then, Barabbas could hear the cries even from inside the stone walls of this fortress.

"Crucify him…crucify him!"

Barabbas shuddered in fear. He would be next. Even now, he heard the sound of heavy boots marching his way. He cowered against the wall, hands shaking, heart beating wildly. He, who had sent many men to uncertain eternities, now careened toward his own. He closed his eyes and saw each of those faces now, drifting across his memory. Men whose families would never see them again presented themselves to him one by pitiful one and then drifted away, as the blood from his blade had slipped away in the creek.

And then other faces floated through his mind.

Adina, Dalia, Hadar.

He feared he would go mad as judgment, wearing Roman boots, marched toward him.

Boots of judgment. Barabbas is in mortal fear of where his choices have led him. What he had meted out to others is now meted out to him. As he watched Jesus dragged away to His execution, coterminous judgment moved inexorably his way.

From a front-row seat in the drama of redemption, Barabbas

is now a star on the stage of eternity, his living death sealed forever if he chooses wrongly. He met the Lord of Glory in his prison, sat next to Him, gripped the same bars, breathed the same air. He knows he has no excuse to avoid the decision thrust upon him.

And neither do we. God will always, always bring every soul to that point of holy confrontation, that abyss where, standing, we view every opportunity we've ever had to reject Him or follow Him. The decision made today will determine where we spend our long tomorrow after we leave this dark world.

The writer of Hebrews leads us to the abyss:

Dear friends, if we deliberately continue sinning after we have received knowledge of the truth, there is no longer any sacrifice that will cover these sins. There is only the terrible expectation of God's judgment and the raging fire that will consume his enemies. For anyone who refused to obey the Law of Moses was put to death without mercy on the testimony of two or three witnesses. Just think how much worse the punishment will be for those who have trampled on the Son of God, and have treated the blood of the covenant, which made us holy, as if it were common and unholy, and have insulted and disdained the Holy Spirit who brings God's mercy to us.
(Hebrews 10:26–29)

Death *with* Jesus is eternal life. Death *without* Him is eternal death—not a merciful oblivion, not partying in hell with all of your friends, not a blissful eternal sleep. It is full, unadulterated life without God—going on and on and on. It is the unending decay of the grave, and the knowledge that one decision, only one, made the difference between heaven and hell.

It is only relationship with the living and eternal Jesus that makes life on earth bearable against the approaching evil, when the full force of wickedness is upon us. Those who reject absolutely the Christ of God will have their way for a time, and what an evil, malevolent time that will be.

Where do you want to be on that day—with Him or without Him?

Barabbas was blinded by the light. He shaded his eyes, tried to focus on the scene before him. Two burly soldiers held him—he could barely stand without their support. He heard, though, the deafening cheers as he came out of the darkness of the prison.

As his eyes adjusted to the blazing sunlight, he saw to his right the judgment seat of Pilate, occupied by the prefect. He looked angry. Before him the masses cheered his, Barabbas's, appearance.

They cheer for me? Why?

The cheers turned to jeers as Jesus appeared on Pilate's balcony, dragged to the opposite side of the judgment seat by no less than twelve armed Roman soldiers. At first Barabbas did not recognize him. Fresh beatings had taken their toll, turning him from a man to a mass of bloody flesh. Barabbas looked away as the soldiers released him and he fell in a heap next to Pilate.

Pilate roused himself and stood.

"I find no cause to execute this man!" he exclaimed loudly, his arm outstretched toward Jesus.

And then gesturing to Barabbas, he exclaimed, "Here is a traitor, a murderer of your own people, a plotter against Rome! Shall I release *him*?"

"Yes!" roared the crowd. "Release him!"

Barabbas couldn't believe his ears. He saw the religious rulers—whom he'd hated and plotted to kill time and again—in the crowd, demanding his release.

Pilate yelled, pointing at Jesus lying at his feet, "And what should I do with this man?"

"Crucify him! Crucify him! Crucify him!" the mob

demanded, each phrase louder and more bloodthirsty than the last.

Pilate shook his head, clearly disbelieving his own ears. He gestured to a servant who carried a basin of water to him. Pilate dipped his hands in the water, ceremoniously washing them, and then raised them high in the air.

"I wash my hands of this! This is on your heads!" he called out.

The crowd responded with, "Yes! We take responsibility! Let us and our children and our grandchildren bear this responsibility! Release Barabbas and crucify the pretender, Jesus!"

"But he is your king," Pilate said.

"We have no king but Caesar!"

The unbelievable words assailed Barabbas's ears.

Were they mad? No king but Caesar? The same Caesar who kept them under his royal thumb year after dismal year, executed random victims on a whim, allowed the taking and ravaging of their women at the will of the garrisons? Have I been transported by the gods to some other world, a world where truth is lie and lies are truth?

Pilate shrugged, and turning from the crowd, he motioned to the soldiers behind Barabbas. Barabbas felt the shackles being taken from his ankles and then a shove to the small of his back. He stood motionless, unsure what was expected of him.

The soldiers picked Jesus up and stood him on his feet. He couldn't stand by himself, so the soldiers held him up. Through swollen eyes, Jesus surveyed the crowd, saying nothing.

A rough voice hissed in Barabbas's ear. "Fool! Get out of here before the prefect changes his mind!"

Galvanized, Barabbas moved toward the steps leading from the dais down to the courtyard. As he reached the steps, he turned back again to look at Jesus. Jesus wasn't looking out at the frenzied throng anymore—his eyes pierced Barabbas's own. They stood, staring at each other over Pilate's head, unmoving. An eerie silence hovered over the unruly gathering.

"Barabbas, will you believe?" came the whispered question.

Gesturing to Pilate, now seated again, Jesus added, "Barabbas, *this* is not the true seat of judgment. This is but a shadow of the real one. This judge has no power to take my life. What say you?"

Barabbas was mute, driven to the edge of madness by the question.

The silence was broken when Pilate waved the soldiers away, with Jesus in tow. Cries of "Crucify him!" followed Jesus down to the street and out to the hill.

Barabbas watched for a moment, and then he turned and ran down the steps, melting into the crowd with Jesus of Nazareth's question burning a hole in his heart.

Do you believe *in* God—or do you *believe God*? Merely believing in God keeps you at a safe distance from Him. You know He's *out there* somewhere, doing His God thing—raising and setting the sun, making rain and snow and thunder, spinning planet earth on its axis—but He's out *there*. He's not up close and personal. There are no questions from Him you have to deal with, no decisions to make, no changes to your life to be considered.

Believing God, however, is a whole different proposition. Believing God requires that you know Him, His nature, His words, and that you spend time learning what He requires of you.

In this story, Barabbas encountered the up-close-and-personal God, stared into His eyes, slept inches from Him, and learned from Him that God desires most of all for His creatures—even a rat—to *know* Him.

The Scriptures do not tell us what Barabbas decided as he ran away. It's probable that he did not change his ways, that he chose not to follow Jesus, that he went back to the life he'd always been living. But maybe not.

Maybe he followed the mob to Golgotha on crucifixion day and beheld the Lord of Glory hanging on the traitor's cross in shame, the cross that should have been Barabbas's own. Perhaps he witnessed that stupendous event, the Creator and Judge of the universe judged and executed by His creatures. If he did, is it possible that it didn't change him?

Barabbas holds the distinction of being the only human ever born for whom Jesus died twice—that day at Golgotha, taking his physical place on a cross—and spiritually, sacrificing Himself so that Barabbas could experience true freedom from sin.

We don't know what Barabbas chose, and we won't until we're on the other side of death.

But Barabbas aside, what about you? God placed Barabbas in a unique place at a unique time so that not only he, but we, would face the same question.

What will you do with Jesus Christ? It's decision time. There will be no chance—after you reject Christ for the last time and take your final earthly breath—to change your mind and slip into heaven under the door.

You will believe God—yes—when you open your eyes in that place, but it will only last a second and then God will disappear from your sight forever. You will spend eternity wishing you'd made the right decision while you drew earthly breath. You will spend eternity reliving all the chances you had, and it will gnaw at you; the knowledge that you put yourself in hell will chew on you, consume you, but it won't send you to oblivion where now you want to be. You will remain alive for all of eternity, knowing you made the worst choice ever, and you will pay for that choice forever. Our loving God does not send us to hell—we ourselves do by the choice to reject His provision in Jesus Christ.

Believe God now—not a religion, not a system of belief—but a Person, a divine relationship. Take Jesus Christ as your personal Lord and Savior now. Get to know Him, read His Word, let *Him* consume you. Then you will spend your forever time knowing Him more and more, His merciful sovereignty and His grace filling you to overflowing.

God doesn't just dwell in the vast, limitless heavens—He inhabits the small spaces of our lives, the hidden, filthy corners, the crevices where we try to hide ourselves and our sins, and He waits for us to see Him there, to ask Him to sweep those spaces clean and open them up to the light of His purpose. If we allow Him, He will bring all our harsh circumstances, our hurts and betrayals, even our own sinful rebellion against Him, into the daylight to be used to draw all people to Him.

There's nothing quite like listening to another's tale of victory over circumstances—circumstances that may sound suspiciously like our own—to bring *us* to the foot of the cross, to give *us* the eternal perspective needed to view our lives from the vantage point of heaven. From those heavenly cliffs, we finally know that no suffering is too much if it brings one more lost soul to glory.

Father, the time for me is now.
I choose to move from believing in You to believing You.

Study Questions—Pardoned

1. Do you think Barabbas decided to believe God that day? Or do you think he went back to his old life? Why?
2. Do you just believe *in* God? Or do you *believe God*? Explain the difference between those two questions in your own words. How does the difference apply to you personally?
3. Contrast the two rats in the story—the one in the hole in which Barabbas was first thrown, and the one Jesus held in his palm. How are they similar, and how are they different?
4. What is the connection between the rats and the "gnawing" knowledge of the unbeliever in hell?
5. What thoughts go through your mind as you contemplate the truth that your sinless Judge became the judged, took your sins with Him to the cross, and then went to hell for you, rising again, leaving your sins behind?